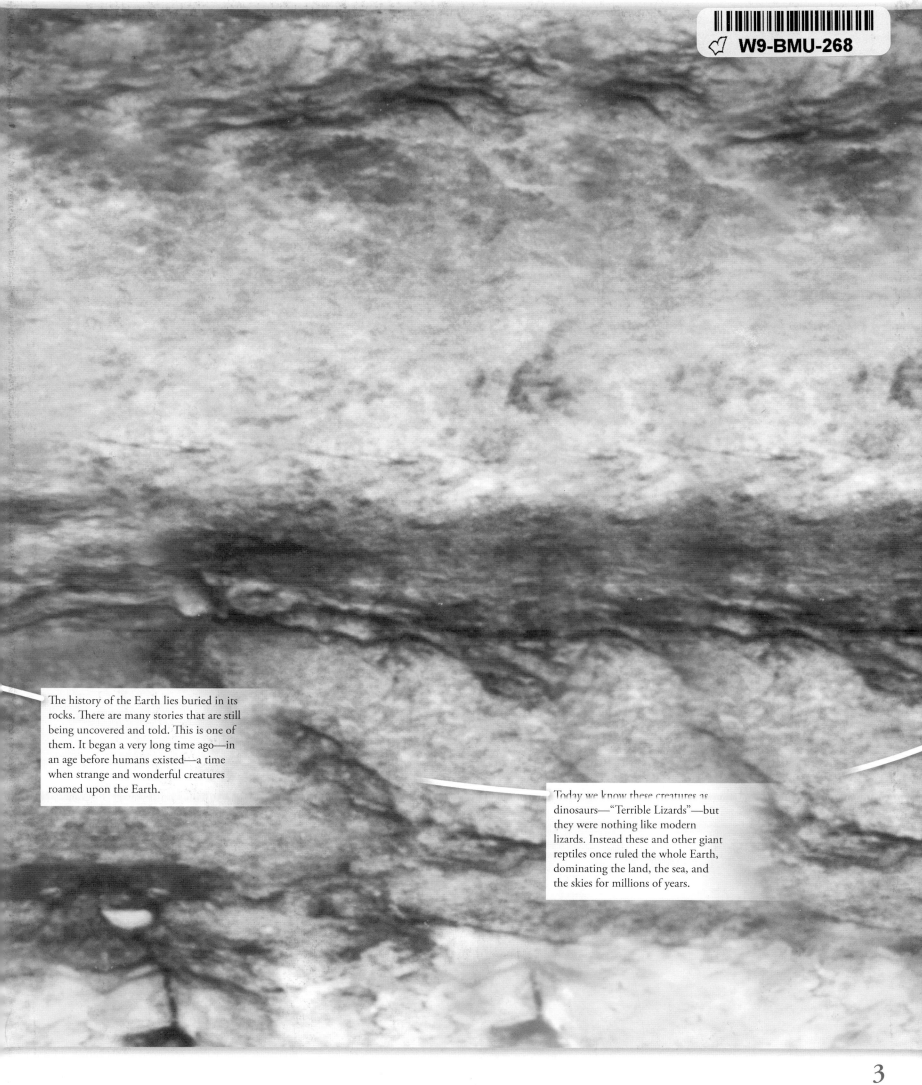

The history of the Earth lies buried in its rocks. There are many stories that are still being uncovered and told. This is one of them. It began a very long time ago—in an age before humans existed—a time when strange and wonderful creatures roamed upon the Earth.

Today we know these creatures as dinosaurs—"Terrible Lizards"—but they were nothing like modern lizards. Instead these and other giant reptiles once ruled the whole Earth, dominating the land, the sea, and the skies for millions of years.

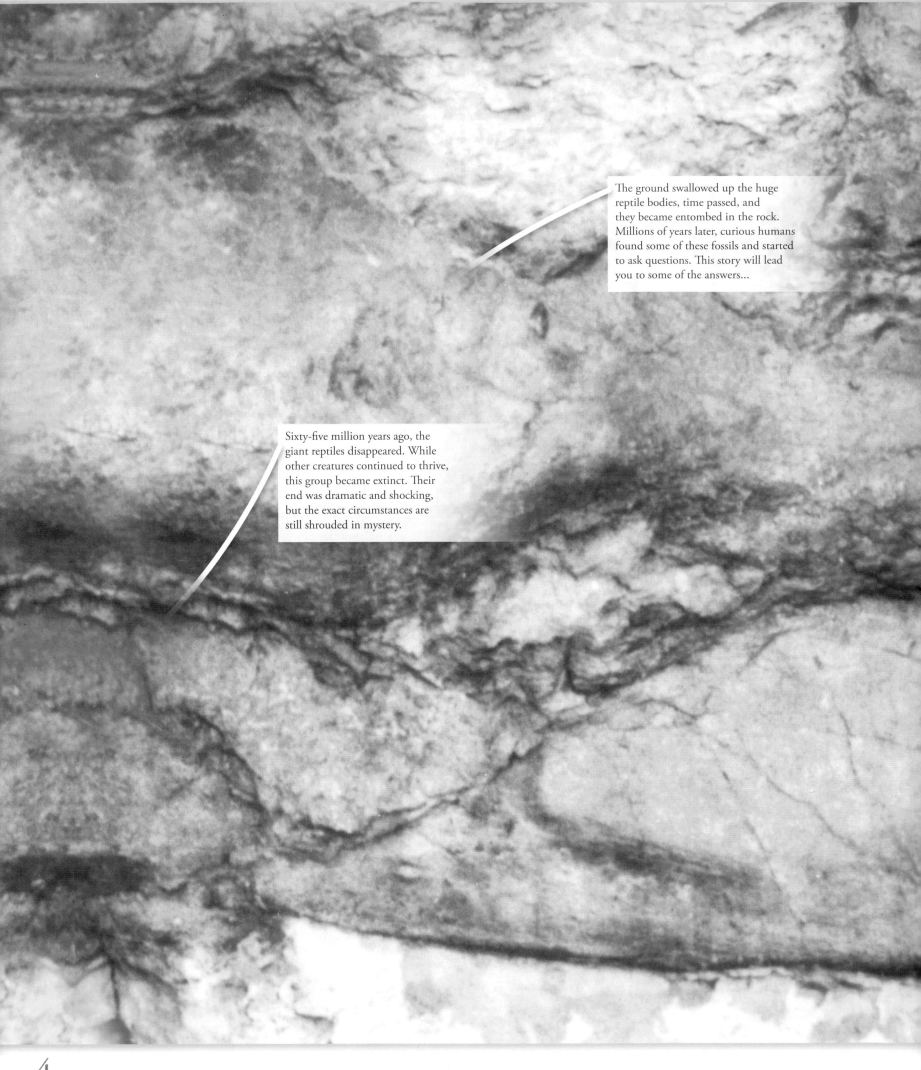

The ground swallowed up the huge reptile bodies, time passed, and they became entombed in the rock. Millions of years later, curious humans found some of these fossils and started to ask questions. This story will lead you to some of the answers...

Sixty-five million years ago, the giant reptiles disappeared. While other creatures continued to thrive, this group became extinct. Their end was dramatic and shocking, but the exact circumstances are still shrouded in mystery.

DK experience
DINOSAUR

written by
JOHN MALAM

THE ROCK GIVES UP ITS SECRETS

DISCOVERY OF *TYRANNOSAURUS REX*

Fossil Finder	
Name	Barnum Brown
Born	1873
Died	1963
Occupation	Paleontologist at the American Museum of Natural History from 1898 to 1942
Famous Find	The first *Tyrannosaurus rex*

Sixty-five million years ago the Earth's climate was hot and the vegetation was lush. Rivers flowed toward a vast inland sea. This was a time when dinosaurs, crocodiles, salamanders, turtles, and small mammals all flourished. When the rivers flooded they spilled across the floodplain and when they shrank back they left behind layers of soft sediment. Some animals wandered into these mud and sand deposits by accident, others were swept there by floodwater—all sank into muddy tombs. As the sediments set hard and became rock, the animal remains turned into fossils. One of them was a *Tyrannosaurus rex*.

Looking for dinosaurs

Fast forward to 1902 and Hell Creek on the banks of the Missouri River, Montana. Dinosaurs had once lived and died here, on a wide floodplain close to an ancient sea. Now it looks very different. As far as the eye can see, the landscape is a wilderness of rocky outcrops and deep canyons. The American Museum of Natural History organized an expedition to survey the area's ancient rocks—rocks that became known as the Hell Creek Beds, rocks that might contain dinosaur fossils. The survey was led by museum paleontologist Barnum Brown.

Dinosaur graveyard

Brown and his team crossed the rugged terrain on horseback. Searching the rocks for clues to ancient life, they found the world's most famous dinosaur. First they discovered a *Triceratops*, but then the bones of an altogether different dinosaur emerged. Brown had never seen anything like them before. Did they belong to an unknown species, one that was new to

science? The only way to find out was to excavate the bones, take them to the museum and piece them together. Heavy blocks of stone—each containing a precious dinosaur fossil—were cut from the bedrock. Horses and wagons moved them to the nearest railroad station, 140 miles (225 km) from the dig site, from where they were taken to New York City. At the museum, the bones were

Barnum Brown (right) excavating a dinosaur fossil.

removed from the rock but only part of the skeleton was there—the rest was still in the ground. The team was very excited when it became clear that the bones belonged to a large, meat-eating dinosaur. Only after Brown recovered more of the creature in 1905 could its full size and appearance be appreciated.

Naming the dinosaur

Bone by bone, the dinosaur's skeleton was slowly rebuilt. At first, it was thought to be *Deinodon horridus* ("Terrible Teeth")—a large carnivore and one of the first dinosaurs to be named in North America. Brown casually referred to his find as the "old *Deinodon* skeleton." As the bones were pieced together, however, it became clear that Brown's dinosaur was not a *Deinodon,* but a new species that would require a name of its own. The task of naming the dinosaur fell to Henry Osborn, the wealthy director of the American Museum of Natural History. Osborn was the first person to describe it, in a famous article written in 1905 for a scientific journal. In it he proposed calling

> *"This is a heavy piece of work but Deinodon bones are so rare that it is worth the work."*
>
> Barnum Brown writing to Henry Osborn in 1905.

the dinosaur *Tyrannosaurus rex* ("King of the Tyrant Lizards"). It was a name the whole world would soon come to know.

The name that got away

What Osborn did not know was that *Tyrannosaurus rex* had already been discovered. In 1892, Edward Drinker Cope had described a single bone from a dinosaur he believed was entirely new. He named the dinosaur *Manospondylus gigas* ("Giant, Thin Vertebra"). Brown's fossils came from the same type of dinosaur, so under the dinosaur-naming rules, the name *Tyrannosaurus rex* should have been abandoned in favor of *Manospondylus.* However, by the time the mistake was discovered, the name of *Tyrannosaurus rex* had become too famous to change.

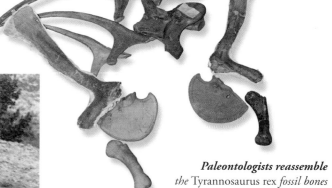

Paleontologists reassemble the Tyrannosaurus rex *fossil bones discovered by Barnum Brown.*

The bones were wrapped in plaster casings to protect them before they were removed from the site.

> "Am now at work on the second large cut in the *Deinodon* quarry, which is 100 feet long, 20 feet deep, 15 feet wide; hard sandstone which has to be blasted before it can be plowed."
>
> Barnum Brown writing to Henry Osborn in 1905.

A CHANGING WORLD

Throughout Earth's very long history, the planet's surface has been shaped by the powerful forces of nature. Some 300 million years ago (mya) all land was joined together in one massive supercontinent known as Pangaea, meaning "All Earth." Then, beginning around 200 million years ago, Pangaea divided into two land masses, **Laurasia** and **Gondwanaland**. Over time, these also broke apart, forming several smaller pieces that became the **continents** we know today. The continents are still on the move, at a rate of nearly 2 in (4 cm) a year—far too slowly for us to notice. The globes here show how Earth's land and sea have changed over time.

Life recovered by the Late Triassic Period (230 to 200 mya), which was when the first dinosaurs appeared—small, two-legged meat-eaters, and larger plant-eaters that walked on two or four legs. All Earth's land was still a part of the Pangaea supercontinent.

In the Early Permian Period of Earth history, 280 million years ago, **reptiles** and **amphibians** were the dominant land animals, roaming across Pangaea. At the end of the Permian Period (251 mya), an estimated 50 percent of all animal life died out.

Pangaea began to crack apart in the Jurassic Period (200 to 144 mya), forming smaller continents separated by sea. The first birds appeared, but reptiles dominated the Earth— **pterosaurs** ruled the skies, and **plesiosaurs** inhabited the sea.

Laurasia The northern half of Pangaea—a landmass made up of North America, Europe, and Asia.

Gondwanaland The southern landmass made up of Africa, Australia, South America, India, and Antarctica.

continents Earth's large landmasses; from a Latin word meaning "continuous land."

reptiles Egg-laying, cold-blooded animals with scales or horny skin, such as lizards.

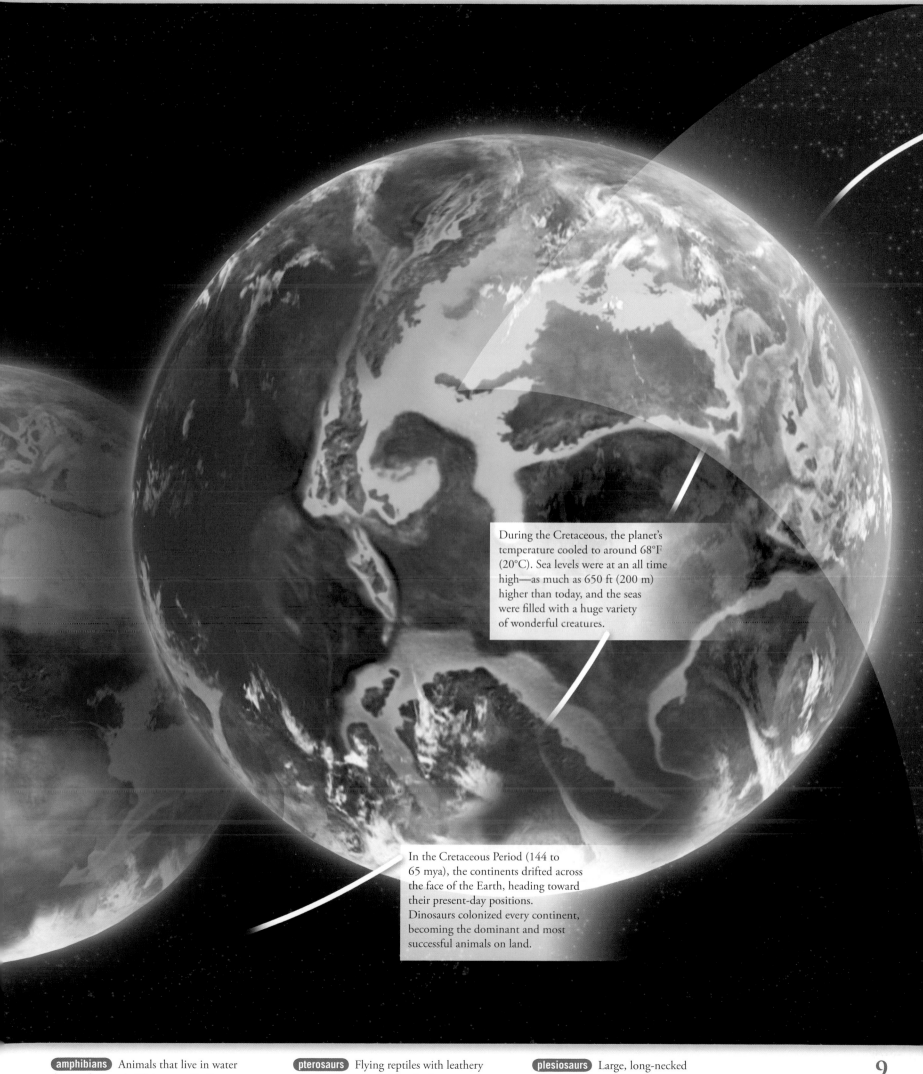

During the Cretaceous, the planet's temperature cooled to around 68°F (20°C). Sea levels were at an all time high—as much as 650 ft (200 m) higher than today, and the seas were filled with a huge variety of wonderful creatures.

In the Cretaceous Period (144 to 65 mya), the continents drifted across the face of the Earth, heading toward their present-day positions. Dinosaurs colonized every continent, becoming the dominant and most successful animals on land.

amphibians Animals that live in water during their early life but usually live on land as adults.

pterosaurs Flying reptiles with leathery wings and bony, toothless beaks.

plesiosaurs Large, long-necked sea reptiles that swam using flipper-shaped limbs.

CRETACEOUS WORLD

Travel back to the Cretaceous Period and you discover a world ruled by reptiles. One group reigned supreme—the dinosaurs. These land-living reptiles were a success story that lasted for millions of years. They roamed over plains, wandered through forests, and gathered at the water's edge. The dinosaurs shared the planet with fish, insects, and small `mammals`. In the skies above were large flying reptiles, whose wings carried them far and wide, but the seas belonged to `predators` that spent their lives below the waves cruising the world's oceans. Although these vast marine reptiles lived in the water, they swam to the surface to breathe air before disappearing back into the deep.

In the Cretaceous ocean it's a case of eat or be eaten. For those at the bottom of the `food chain`, survival is all about self-defense, while predators higher up in the eating order depend on their skills as hunters.

A fish uses its maneuverability and speed to flee from predators, but when an *Elasmosaurus*, or "Plate Lizard," is on its tail, its chances of escape are slim. This long-necked plesiosaur searches the oceans for fish, squid, and spiral-shelled `ammonites`.

Of all Cretaceous marine reptiles, `mosasaurs` are the fiercest predators, and *Tylosaurus*, or "Swollen Lizard," is the most awesome of all. Its long, slender body is propelled through the water by its powerful tail, which it swishes from side to side.

Elasmosaurus has a snakelike neck about 23 ft (7 m) long. It chases after its `prey`, matching the creature's attempts to escape with twists and turns of its neck. Or it waits for a shoal of fish to swim by, then plunges its head and starts fishing.

`mammals` Animals that give birth to live young and produce milk to feed them.

`predators` Animals that hunt and kill other animals for food.

`food chain` The feeding order—each link in the chain feeds on a lower member and is food for the link above them.

`ammonites` Early shell creatures that lived in the sea and became extinct at the same time as the dinosaurs.

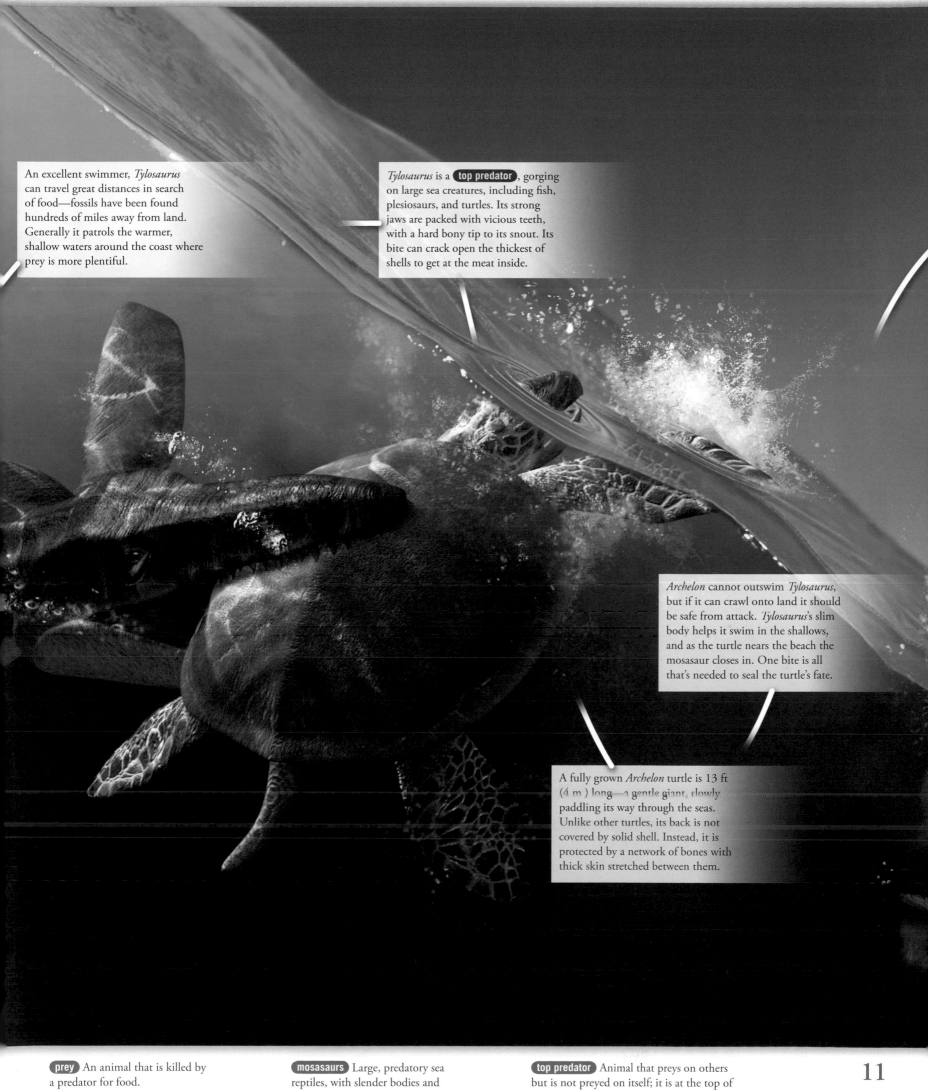

An excellent swimmer, *Tylosaurus* can travel great distances in search of food—fossils have been found hundreds of miles away from land. Generally it patrols the warmer, shallow waters around the coast where prey is more plentiful.

Tylosaurus is a **top predator**, gorging on large sea creatures, including fish, plesiosaurs, and turtles. Its strong jaws are packed with vicious teeth, with a hard bony tip to its snout. Its bite can crack open the thickest of shells to get at the meat inside.

Archelon cannot outswim *Tylosaurus*, but if it can crawl onto land it should be safe from attack. *Tylosaurus*'s slim body helps it swim in the shallows, and as the turtle nears the beach the mosasaur closes in. One bite is all that's needed to seal the turtle's fate.

A fully grown *Archelon* turtle is 13 ft (4 m) long—a gentle giant, slowly paddling its way through the seas. Unlike other turtles, its back is not covered by solid shell. Instead, it is protected by a network of bones with thick skin stretched between them.

prey An animal that is killed by a predator for food.

mosasaurs Large, predatory sea reptiles, with slender bodies and flipper-shaped limbs.

top predator Animal that preys on others but is not preyed on itself; it is at the top of the food chain.

11

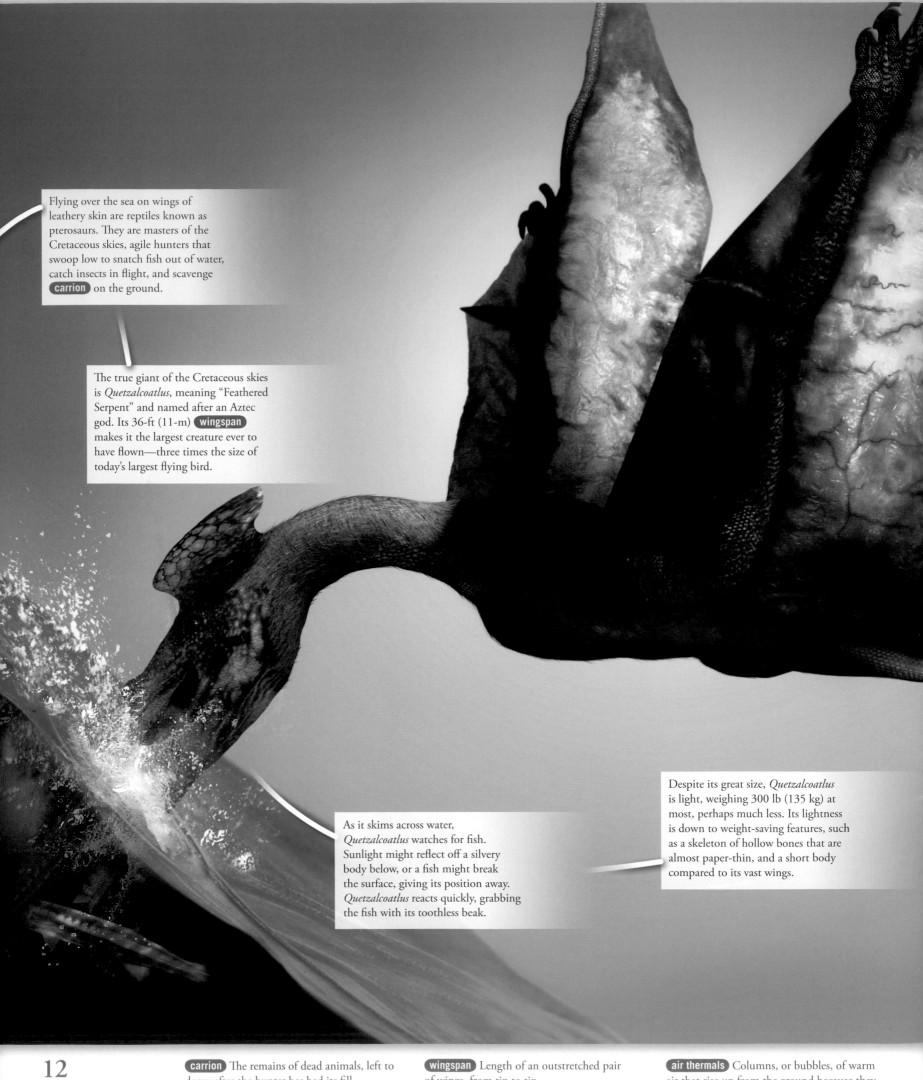

Flying over the sea on wings of leathery skin are reptiles known as pterosaurs. They are masters of the Cretaceous skies, agile hunters that swoop low to snatch fish out of water, catch insects in flight, and scavenge **carrion** on the ground.

The true giant of the Cretaceous skies is *Quetzalcoatlus*, meaning "Feathered Serpent" and named after an Aztec god. Its 36-ft (11-m) **wingspan** makes it the largest creature ever to have flown—three times the size of today's largest flying bird.

As it skims across water, *Quetzalcoatlus* watches for fish. Sunlight might reflect off a silvery body below, or a fish might break the surface, giving its position away. *Quetzalcoatlus* reacts quickly, grabbing the fish with its toothless beak.

Despite its great size, *Quetzalcoatlus* is light, weighing 300 lb (135 kg) at most, perhaps much less. Its lightness is down to weight-saving features, such as a skeleton of hollow bones that are almost paper-thin, and a short body compared to its vast wings.

carrion The remains of dead animals, left to decay after the hunter has had its fill.

wingspan Length of an outstretched pair of wings, from tip to tip.

air thermals Columns, or bubbles, of warm air that rise up from the ground because they are lighter than the cold air above them.

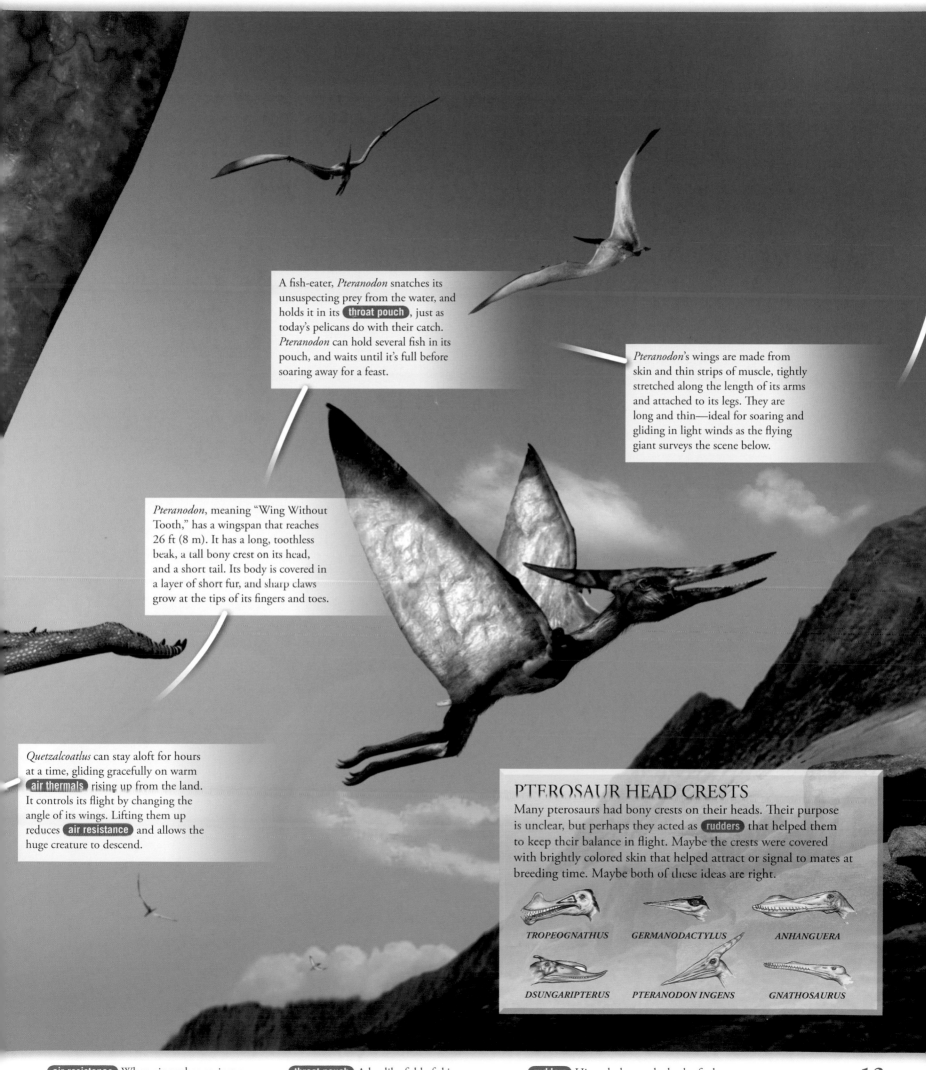

A fish-eater, *Pteranodon* snatches its unsuspecting prey from the water, and holds it in its throat pouch, just as today's pelicans do with their catch. *Pteranodon* can hold several fish in its pouch, and waits until it's full before soaring away for a feast.

Pteranodon's wings are made from skin and thin strips of muscle, tightly stretched along the length of its arms and attached to its legs. They are long and thin—ideal for soaring and gliding in light winds as the flying giant surveys the scene below.

Pteranodon, meaning "Wing Without Tooth," has a wingspan that reaches 26 ft (8 m). It has a long, toothless beak, a tall bony crest on its head, and a short tail. Its body is covered in a layer of short fur, and sharp claws grow at the tips of its fingers and toes.

Quetzalcoatlus can stay aloft for hours at a time, gliding gracefully on warm air thermals rising up from the land. It controls its flight by changing the angle of its wings. Lifting them up reduces air resistance and allows the huge creature to descend.

PTEROSAUR HEAD CRESTS

Many pterosaurs had bony crests on their heads. Their purpose is unclear, but perhaps they acted as rudders that helped them to keep their balance in flight. Maybe the crests were covered with brightly colored skin that helped attract or signal to mates at breeding time. Maybe both of these ideas are right.

TROPEOGNATHUS   GERMANODACTYLUS   ANHANGUERA

DSUNGARIPTERUS   PTERANODON INGENS   GNATHOSAURUS

air resistance When air pushes against a moving object, slowing it down.

throat pouch A baglike fold of skin on the throat where food is held until the animal is ready to eat.

rudders Hinged plate at the back of a boat or plane, used to help direct its course.

13

The land in the Cretaceous is dominated by dinosaurs, thriving in tropical and subtropical temperatures. Dense forests give way to open spaces covered with low-growing plants, and water runs off nearby hills into rivers and pools.

New forms of dinosaur appear in this period. **Hadrosaurs**, or duck-billed dinosaurs, such as *Maiasaura*, meaning "Good Mother Lizard," roam across open countryside, perhaps in herds of thousands of animals. These are docile **herbivores**, or plant-eaters.

Some dinosaurs develop weapons for self-defense. *Triceratops*, which means "Three-Horned Face," is a large, bulky **ceratopsian**, or horned dinosaur. It has a protective shield of bone at the back of its head, and three sharp horns at the front.

Packs of meat-eating dinosaurs, such as *Dromaeosaurus* or "Running Lizard," stalk the herds, waiting for their chance to attack a stray *Maiasaura*. They are smaller than the hadrosaur, but much faster and armed with flesh-ripping claws and teeth.

hadrosaurs Large dinosaurs, with wide, flat beaks, that ate plants; also called duck-bills.

herbivores Animals that eat only plants, as opposed to carnivores—animals that eat other animals.

ceratopsian A large, plant-eating dinosaur with pointed horns and a bony frill growing from the back of its skull.

CRETACEOUS PLANTS

In North America, the late Cretaceous world (about 100–65 million years ago) was a landscape of forests and open plains. Oak, maple, walnut, beech, and magnolia trees flourished. These were new, broad-leaved varieties, growing alongside the evergreen cone-bearing conifers, tree ferns, and ancient palmlike trees called cycads. The ground was carpeted with ferns, not grass, which did not exist at the time of the dinosaurs.

Magnolia

Oak

Maple

Ankylosaurus, meaning "Stiff Lizards," is an **ankylosaur**, or armored dinosaur. Its body is covered in oval, bony plates and spikes, and its long tail ends in a heavy, knobbly club that can do serious damage to an attacker.

The air buzzes with insects. Brightly colored dragonflies with 6-in (15-cm) wingspans patrol their **hunting ranges**, searching for prey. Formidable predators, they catch insects in flight. It's a nonstop battle for survival, even for the smallest.

Dinosaurs may be the dominant animal group on land, but they do not have it all to themselves. Early species of mammals start to appear at this time. *Alphadon* or "First Tooth," is a small, tree-dwelling, fur-covered **marsupial**.

ankylosaur A plant-eating armored dinosaur covered with bony plates, knobs, and spikes.

marsupial Mammals with pouches—the females have pouches to carry their young until they are fully developed.

hunting ranges Areas over which predatory animals search for their prey.

KING OF THE DINOSAURS

At the very end of the Cretaceous Period, the part of the world where North America is today was home to *Tyrannosaurus rex*. It was not the biggest meat-eating dinosaur (that honor belongs to the *Giganotosaurus* or "Giant Southern Lizard" of South America), but it was the first of the massive flesh-eaters to be found. Since its discovery in 1902, *Tyrannosaurus rex* has become the world's most famous dinosaur, yet our knowledge of it is based on only a few adult specimens. No fossils of *Tyrannosaurus rex* **juveniles**, babies, or eggs have been found yet. Despite this lack of evidence, it is possible to piece together its **life cycle**, with help from other dinosaur **fossils** and modern reptiles.

Imagine a clearing between the trees. Weak sunlight filters through the leaf canopy and strikes the ground, making dappled patterns of light and dark. Low-growing plants live in this shady, cool twilight zone. Something else values this secluded glade, too.

The ground is covered in lumps and bumps. They look like giant molehills, but they're not. The mounds seem to be old. Dead vegetation is scattered all around them. It looks like something dug into the mounds or crawled out of them.

The nest is a shallow scoop in the ground, into which the mother has laid her eggs. She's covered them with a mound of leaves, twigs, bark, moss, and dung. The covering hides and protects the eggs, and as it rots it makes heat.

MOTHER AND FATHER

When a female *Tyrannosaurus rex* was ready to breed, she probably released pheromones—chemicals secreted into the air—to attract a mate. Her skin tone may have changed color, another signal that she was looking for a partner. The female was larger than the male. It might have been his job to build the nest and guard the female until she had laid her eggs. If other males came close, he would have chased them away. Once the eggs had been laid, perhaps the male left the nest site. The female stayed with the nest.

One mound is in use, and standing guard beside it is the owner—a masssive female *Tyrannosaurus rex*. The mound is her nest, measuring about 3–6 ft (1–2 m) across, and deep inside it is a **clutch** of 10 eggs, each one a tyrannosaur in the making.

juveniles The young of an animal species, midway between babies and adults.

life cycle The stages of an animal's (or plant's) life, from birth to death.

fossils Part of a dead plant or animal that has been buried and has been turned as hard as stone by minerals in the rock.

Every few minutes the mother pushes her snout into the nest. If it feels too cold, she piles on more vegetation to keep the heat inside. If it's too hot, she opens the nest to let heat escape. She instinctively knows what the temperature should be.

The eggs are long and oval, with cream-colored shells covered in tiny pits, like the skin of an orange. We can only guess at their size but judging by other dinosaur eggs, they could be at least 12 in (30 cm)— about the size of a football.

Inside their safe, warm, stinking nest, the eggs slowly incubate, until they are ready to hatch. The mother stays by her nest; it is her duty to guard its precious contents. She does not sit on the nest, as birds do, or she would crush her eggs.

clutch A set of eggs laid at the same time in the same nest.

incubate To stay warm and in favourable conditions for animals to develop and grow inside the eggs.

snout A long projecting nose and jaws.

The eggshell is **porous**, allowing air to pass through it to the baby inside. If the shell is too thick, the baby will not be able to breathe and will die. If it's too thin, the egg might break. It has to be just the right thickness for the baby to survive and grow.

Inside the egg, the baby tyrannosaur, or **embryo**, is tightly curled up. It will be twice the length of the egg at hatching. As the embryo develops, it absorbs the **yolk** of the egg, which is the dinosaur's only food supply until it hatches from its shell.

A small bump grows on the tip of the baby dinosaur's snout. It's an egg tooth that the baby tyrannosaur will use to crack open the shell when it's time for it to hatch. Modern birds and crocodiles use egg teeth to break out of their shells, too.

Eggs kept warm hatch sooner than cool ones. No one knows how long the incubation period was for *Tyrannosaurus rex*, but based on present-day reptiles, such as crocodiles, it might have been between 60 and 80 days.

18

porous Allowing air or liquid to pass through.

embryo An unborn baby growing inside an egg, or in the womb inside its mother.

yolk The yellow part inside an egg that feeds the growing embryo.

When the mother tyrannosaur returns, her hungry babies' mouths open wide to accept the morsels of food she brings for them. They gain weight quickly, and soon it will be time for them to take their first steps away from the nest.

The baby dinosaurs stay in the nest. It's a dangerous time for them. While their mother is away searching for food, they lie low and keep quiet. If they draw attention to themselves, a predator might seize the chance for a snatch-and-grab attack.

The young emerge within a day or so of each other. This way they will all have the same chances of survival. Any that hatch late will be in danger. They will be the weakest ones, and might be ignored by their mother, or eaten by the bigger hatchlings.

BABY FOSSIL

Fossils of dinosaur embryos are ultrarare. One was discovered in China in 1995, curled up inside an 18-in (45-cm) egg. The dinosaur, nicknamed "Baby Louie," was found with three other unhatched eggs, laid by an **oviraptor** about 70 million years ago.

"Baby Louie" dinosaur embryo

oviraptor A long-legged, beaked, birdlike dinosaur.

FLUFFY TYRANNOSAURS?

As each new tyrannosaur fossil is unearthed, fresh information about these dinosaurs comes to light. In recent years, it has become clear that some **theropods** had feathers—or featherlike growths—on their bodies. Together with their hollow bones, these dinosaurs clearly had something in common with birds. Fossils of one **species** of tyrannosaur from China (*Dilong paradoxus*) show that it had a feathery coat, so it is likely that *Tyrannosaurus rex* had a fuzz of small feathers over it.

Feathery imprint visible above the bone

Chinese fossil

The infants demand food, and their mother sees to it that they are fed. She brings meat for them, dropping chunks onto the ground for them to eat. They sink their tiny teeth into it, and jerk their heads to pull off bite-sized pieces.

As the baby tyrannosaurs grow, their confidence increases and they begin to wander a short distance from the nest. Being small, they are vulnerable to predators. At the first hint of danger they run back to their mother, or take shelter in the undergrowth.

Death is never far away at this tender age and only the fittest will survive **infancy**. Despite being brothers and sisters, they are also rivals, and when it comes to food, the strong take from the weak. Starvation can claim the lives of many baby dinosaurs.

theropods A group of dinosaurs that includes all carnivores. Most were bipedal—walking on two legs, like *Tyrannosaurus rex*.

species A group of similar animals (or plants).

infancy The early childhood stage of an animal's development.

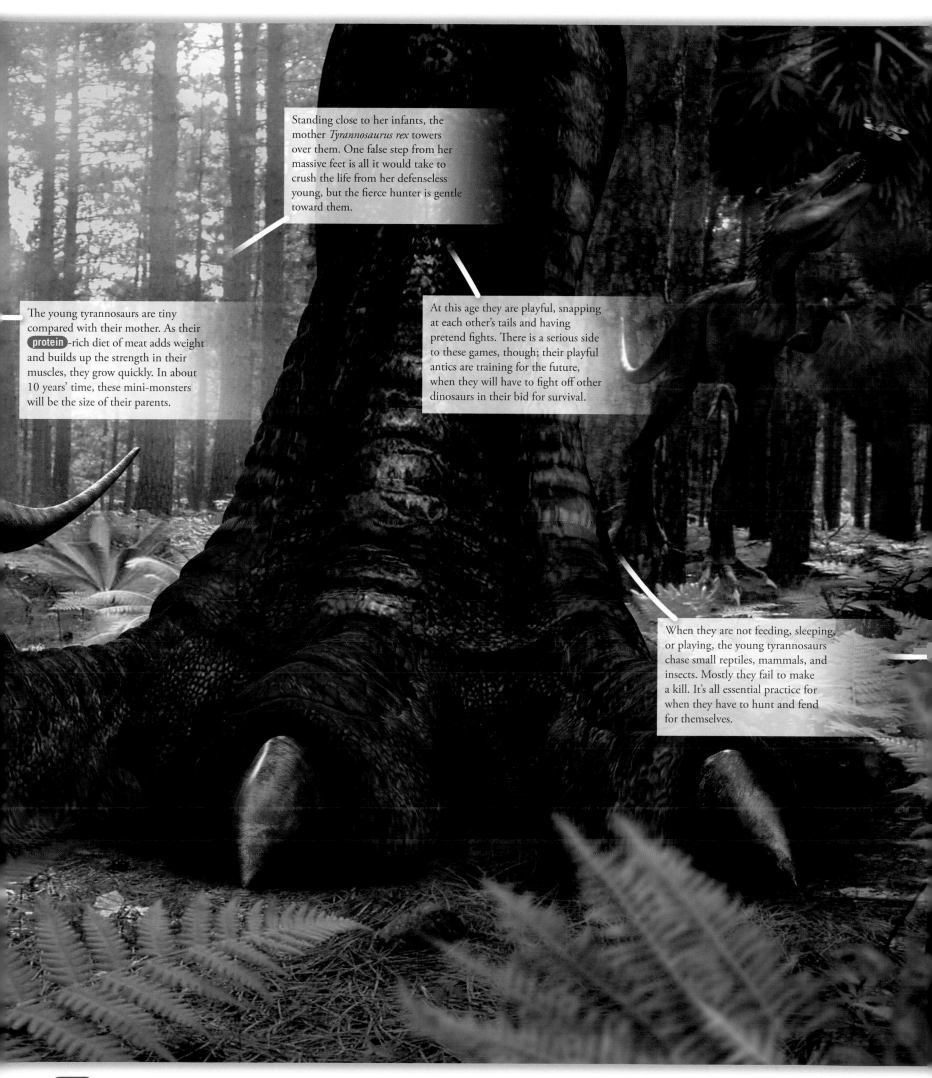

Standing close to her infants, the mother *Tyrannosaurus rex* towers over them. One false step from her massive feet is all it would take to crush the life from her defenseless young, but the fierce hunter is gentle toward them.

The young tyrannosaurs are tiny compared with their mother. As their protein-rich diet of meat adds weight and builds up the strength in their muscles, they grow quickly. In about 10 years' time, these mini-monsters will be the size of their parents.

At this age they are playful, snapping at each other's tails and having pretend fights. There is a serious side to these games, though; their playful antics are training for the future, when they will have to fight off other dinosaurs in their bid for survival.

When they are not feeding, sleeping, or playing, the young tyrannosaurs chase small reptiles, mammals, and insects. Mostly they fail to make a kill. It's all essential practice for when they have to hunt and fend for themselves.

protein An essential type of food for animals. Protein is found in meat, fish, eggs, and milk.

CATALOG OF *T. REX* FOSSILS

Our knowledge of *Tyrannosaurus rex* is based entirely on fossil evidence. By reconstructing its bones, we can gain a pretty good understanding of its likely appearance and habits. However, many details are still unclear. Where no definite evidence has yet been found, paleontologists make "best guesses" from the fossil evidence of other dinosaurs. Here are some of the key features of *Tyrannosaurus rex* and the evidence for them.

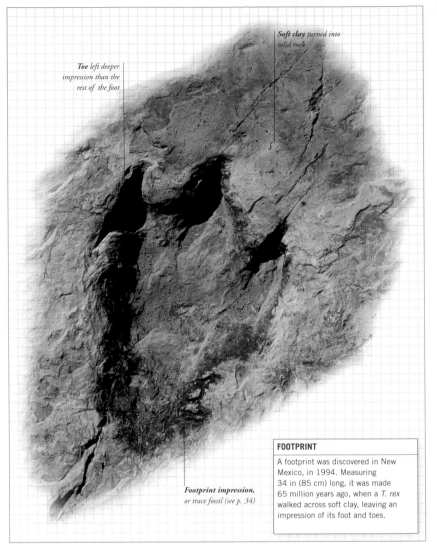

Soft clay turned into solid rock

Toe left deeper impression than the rest of the foot

Footprint impression, or trace fossil (see p. 34)

FOOTPRINT

A footprint was discovered in New Mexico, in 1994. Measuring 34 in (85 cm) long, it was made 65 million years ago, when a *T. rex* walked across soft clay, leaving an impression of its foot and toes.

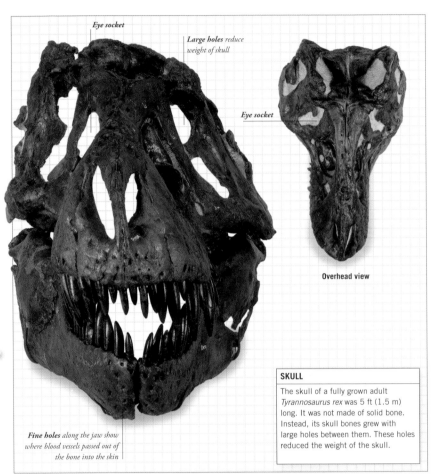

Eye socket

Large holes *reduce weight of skull*

Eye socket

Overhead view

Fine holes *along the jaw show where blood vessels passed out of the bone into the skin*

SKULL

The skull of a fully grown adult *Tyrannosaurus rex* was 5 ft (1.5 m) long. It was not made of solid bone. Instead, its skull bones grew with large holes between them. These holes reduced the weight of the skull.

Largest *dinosaur coprolite ever found*

COPROLITE

A huge coprolite (fossilized dung) was discovered in Saskatchewan, Canada, in 1995. It measured 17 in (44 cm) long and contained bone fragments, proving it came from a meat-eater, probably a *Tyrannosaurus rex*.

RECREATING THE SKULL SHAPE

Computerized axial tomography (CAT) scanning is used to create a three-dimensional (3-D) image from a series of X-rays. On the right is a 3-D scan of a compressed *T. rex* skull. On the left is the skull recreated in its original shape using 3-D CAT scan technology.

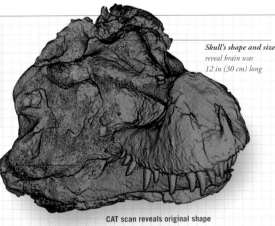

Skull *expanded vertically to show its original proportions*

CAT scan reveals original shape

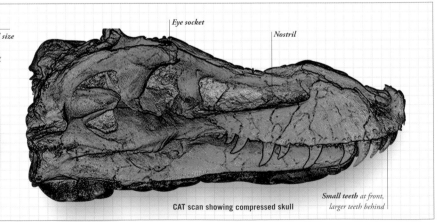

Skull's shape and size *reveal brain was 12 in (30 cm) long*

Eye socket

Nostril

Small teeth *at front, larger teeth behind*

CAT scan showing compressed skull

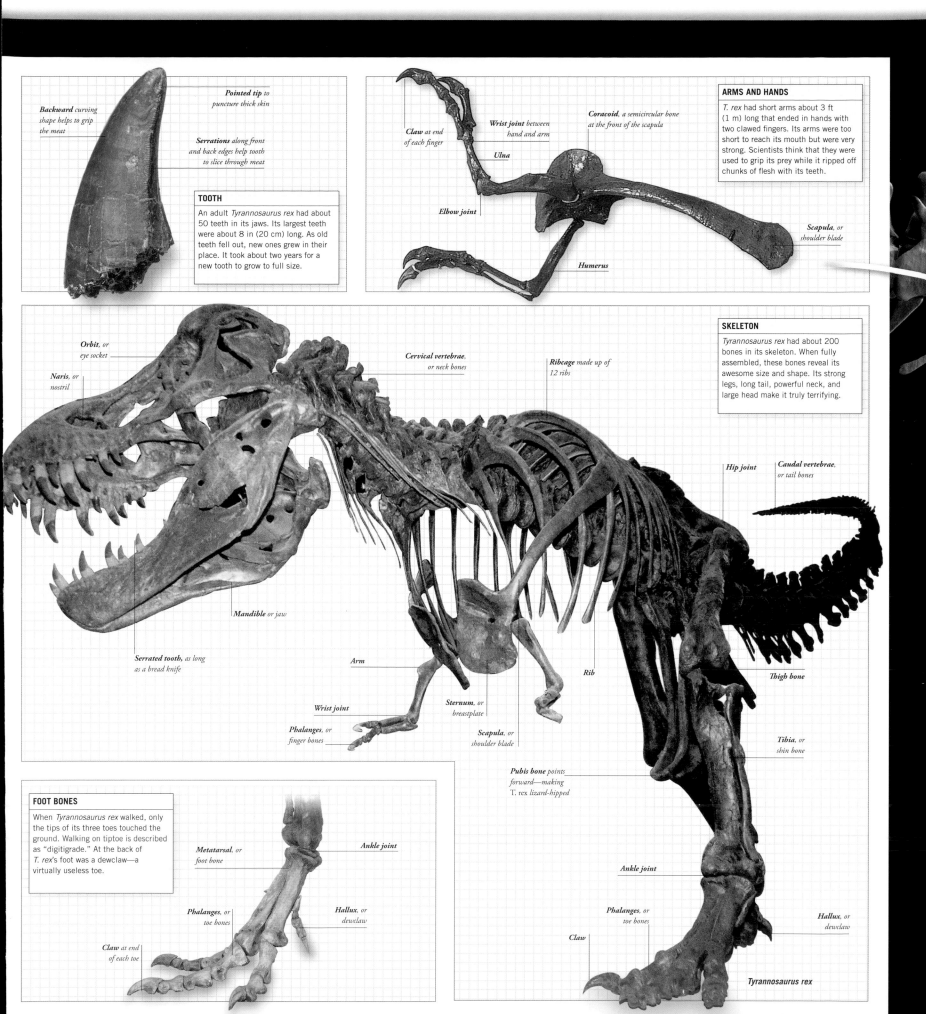

Backward curving shape helps to grip the meat

Pointed tip to puncture thick skin

Serrations along front and back edges help tooth to slice through meat

TOOTH

An adult *Tyrannosaurus rex* had about 50 teeth in its jaws. Its largest teeth were about 8 in (20 cm) long. As old teeth fell out, new ones grew in their place. It took about two years for a new tooth to grow to full size.

Claw at end of each finger

Wrist joint between hand and arm

Coracoid, a semicircular bone at the front of the scapula

Ulna

Elbow joint

Humerus

Scapula, or shoulder blade

ARMS AND HANDS

T. rex had short arms about 3 ft (1 m) long that ended in hands with two clawed fingers. Its arms were too short to reach its mouth but were very strong. Scientists think that they were used to grip its prey while it ripped off chunks of flesh with its teeth.

SKELETON

Tyrannosaurus rex had about 200 bones in its skeleton. When fully assembled, these bones reveal its awesome size and shape. Its strong legs, long tail, powerful neck, and large head make it truly terrifying.

Orbit, or eye socket

Naris, or nostril

Cervical vertebrae, or neck bones

Ribcage made up of 12 ribs

Hip joint

Caudal vertebrae, or tail bones

Mandible or jaw

Serrated tooth, as long as a bread knife

Arm

Rib

Thigh bone

Wrist joint

Sternum, or breastplate

Scapula, or shoulder blade

Phalanges, or finger bones

Tibia, or shin bone

Pubis bone points forward—making *T. rex* lizard-hipped

FOOT BONES

When *Tyrannosaurus rex* walked, only the tips of its three toes touched the ground. Walking on tiptoe is described as "digitigrade." At the back of *T. rex*'s foot was a dewclaw—a virtually useless toe.

Metatarsal, or foot bone

Ankle joint

Ankle joint

Phalanges, or toe bones

Hallux, or dewclaw

Phalanges, or toe bones

Hallux, or dewclaw

Claw at end of each toe

Claw

Tyrannosaurus rex

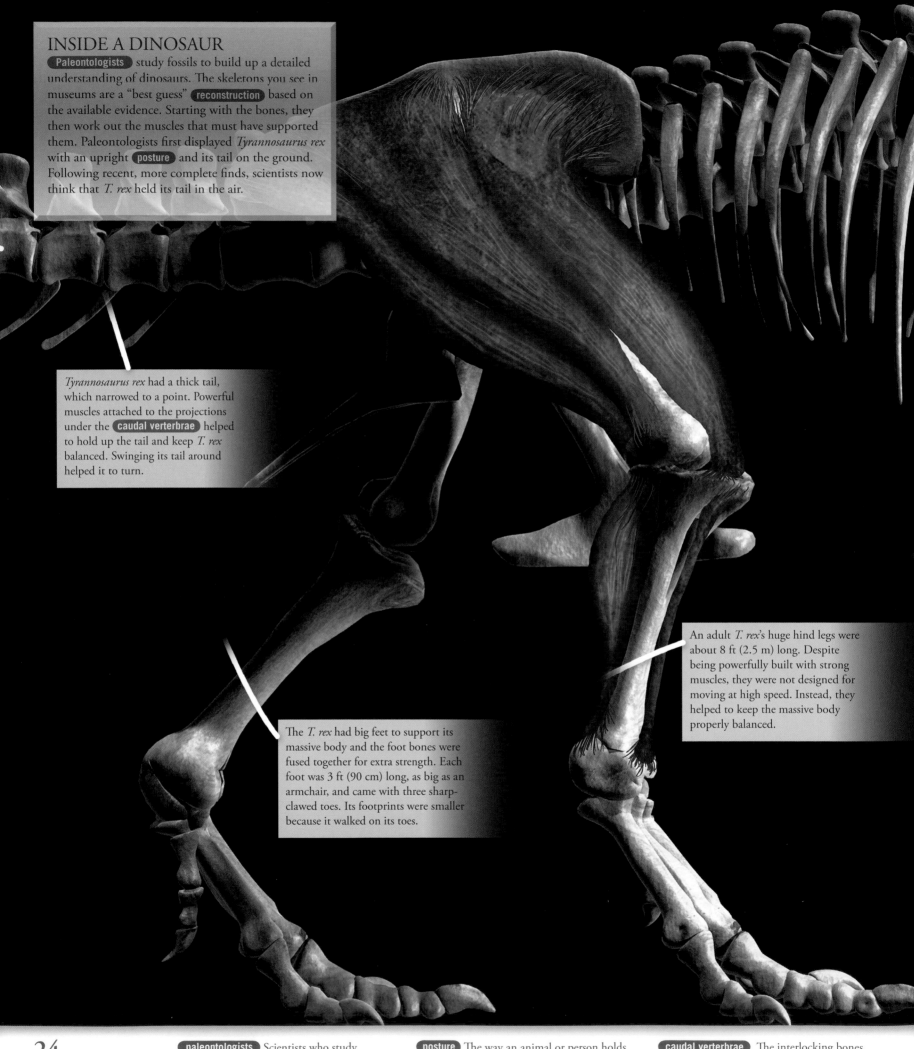

INSIDE A DINOSAUR

Paleontologists study fossils to build up a detailed understanding of dinosaurs. The skeletons you see in museums are a "best guess" reconstruction based on the available evidence. Starting with the bones, they then work out the muscles that must have supported them. Paleontologists first displayed *Tyrannosaurus rex* with an upright posture and its tail on the ground. Following recent, more complete finds, scientists now think that *T. rex* held its tail in the air.

Tyrannosaurus rex had a thick tail, which narrowed to a point. Powerful muscles attached to the projections under the caudal verterbrae helped to hold up the tail and keep *T. rex* balanced. Swinging its tail around helped it to turn.

An adult *T. rex*'s huge hind legs were about 8 ft (2.5 m) long. Despite being powerfully built with strong muscles, they were not designed for moving at high speed. Instead, they helped to keep the massive body properly balanced.

The *T. rex* had big feet to support its massive body and the foot bones were fused together for extra strength. Each foot was 3 ft (90 cm) long, as big as an armchair, and came with three sharp-clawed toes. Its footprints were smaller because it walked on its toes.

paleontologists Scientists who study life-forms that existed in previous geological periods, mainly through studying fossils.

posture The way an animal or person holds its body when it stands or moves.

caudal verterbrae The interlocking bones that make up the tail.

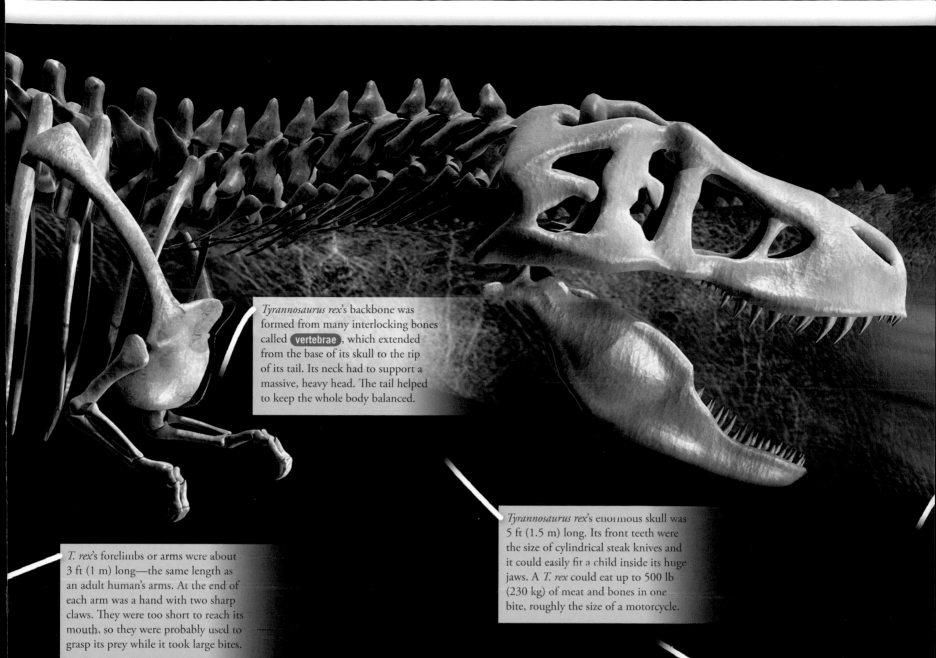

Tyrannosaurus rex's backbone was formed from many interlocking bones called **vertebrae**, which extended from the base of its skull to the tip of its tail. Its neck had to support a massive, heavy head. The tail helped to keep the whole body balanced.

T. rex's forelimbs or arms were about 3 ft (1 m) long—the same length as an adult human's arms. At the end of each arm was a hand with two sharp claws. They were too short to reach its mouth, so they were probably used to grasp its prey while it took large bites.

Tyrannosaurus rex's enormous skull was 5 ft (1.5 m) long. Its front teeth were the size of cylindrical steak knives and it could easily fit a child inside its huge jaws. A *T. rex* could eat up to 500 lb (230 kg) of meat and bones in one bite, roughly the size of a motorcycle.

Reconstructions of *Tyrannosaurus rex* skeletons show that a fully grown adult measured about 42 ft (12.8 m) from snout to tail and stood about 13 ft (4 m) high at the hips. With flesh and organs added, its "live" weight would have been around 7 tons.

FAST OR SLOW?

Paleontologists have calculated a **stride** for *Tyrannosaurus rex* of 12–15 ft (3.7–4.6 m). From this they have calculated a walking speed of about 7½ mph (12 kph) and a top speed of about 22 mph (36 kph). They once thought it could run faster than this, but detailed studies of its legs show that this would not have been possible. To move at higher speeds, *Tyrannosaurus rex* would have needed much larger leg muscles than it actually had. But then it would have weighed too much to move at all.

---

reconstruction A mounted skeleton that shows its scale and structure. A restoration shows how a dinosaur might have looked when it was alive.

stride The distance measured between the toes of each foot while walking or running.

vertebrae The interlocking bones that make up the spine or backbone.

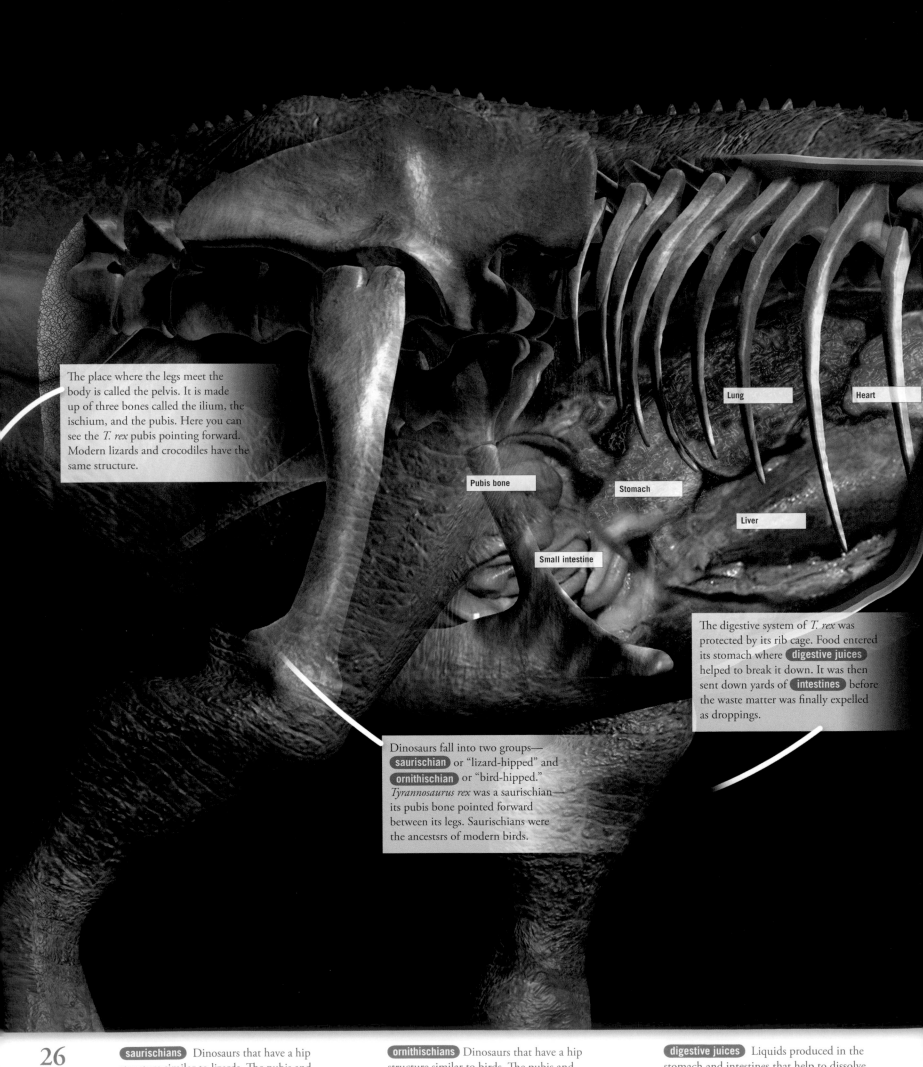

The place where the legs meet the body is called the pelvis. It is made up of three bones called the ilium, the ischium, and the pubis. Here you can see the *T. rex* pubis pointing forward. Modern lizards and crocodiles have the same structure.

Lung

Heart

Pubis bone

Stomach

Liver

Small intestine

The digestive system of *T. rex* was protected by its rib cage. Food entered its stomach where **digestive juices** helped to break it down. It was then sent down yards of **intestines** before the waste matter was finally expelled as droppings.

Dinosaurs fall into two groups—**saurischian** or "lizard-hipped" and **ornithischian** or "bird-hipped." *Tyrannosaurus rex* was a saurischian—its pubis bone pointed forward between its legs. Saurischians were the ancestsrs of modern birds.

saurischians Dinosaurs that have a hip structure similar to lizards. The pubis and ischium point in opposite directions.

ornithischians Dinosaurs that have a hip structure similar to birds. The pubis and ischium both point backward.

digestive juices Liquids produced in the stomach and intestines that help to dissolve food as it passes through the body.

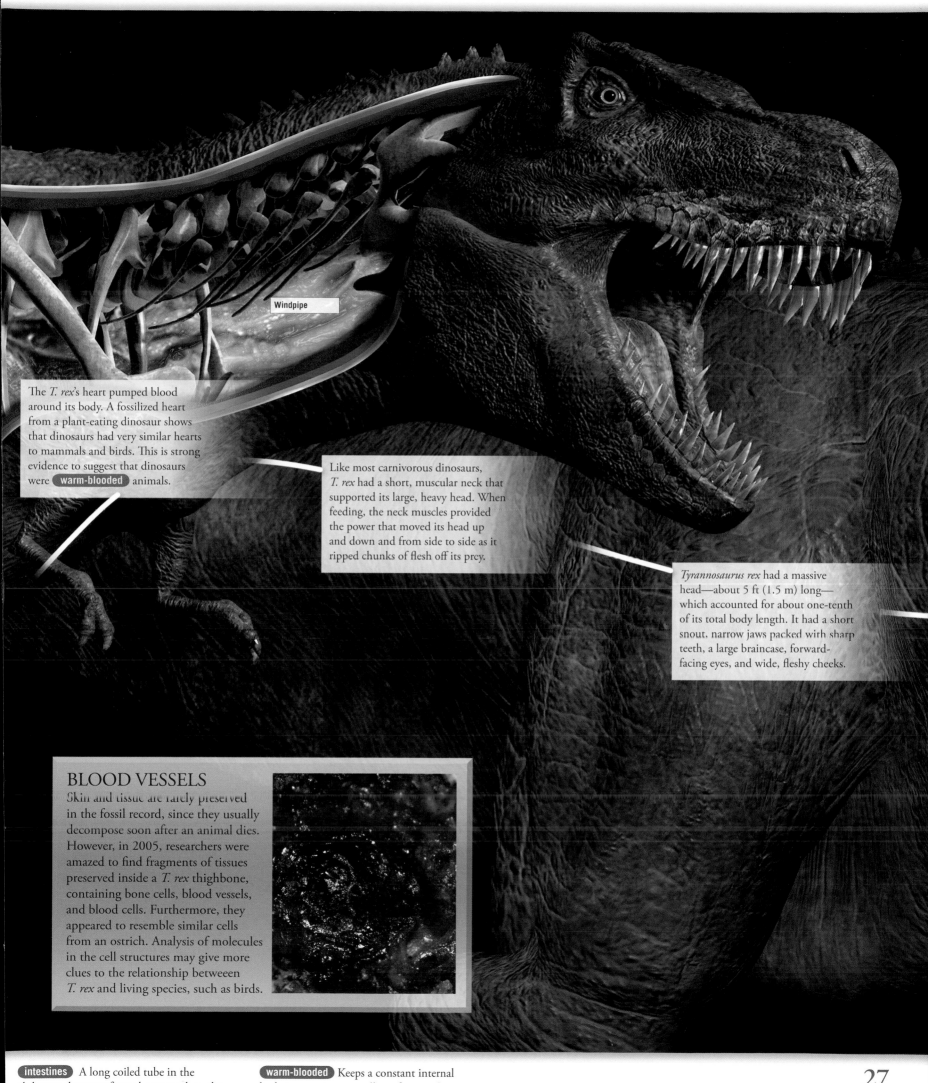

Windpipe

The *T. rex*'s heart pumped blood around its body. A fossilized heart from a plant-eating dinosaur shows that dinosaurs had very similar hearts to mammals and birds. This is strong evidence to suggest that dinosaurs were **warm-blooded** animals.

Like most carnivorous dinosaurs, *T. rex* had a short, muscular neck that supported its large, heavy head. When feeding, the neck muscles provided the power that moved its head up and down and from side to side as it ripped chunks of flesh off its prey.

Tyrannosaurus rex had a massive head—about 5 ft (1.5 m) long— which accounted for about one-tenth of its total body length. It had a short snout, narrow jaws packed with sharp teeth, a large braincase, forward-facing eyes, and wide, fleshy cheeks.

BLOOD VESSELS

Skin and tissue are rarely preserved in the fossil record, since they usually decompose soon after an animal dies. However, in 2005, researchers were amazed to find fragments of tissues preserved inside a *T. rex* thighbone, containing bone cells, blood vessels, and blood cells. Furthermore, they appeared to resemble similar cells from an ostrich. Analysis of molecules in the cell structures may give more clues to the relationship between *T. rex* and living species, such as birds.

intestines A long coiled tube in the abdomen that runs from the stomach to the anus and digests and absorbs food and water.

warm-blooded Keeps a constant internal body temperature regardless of external conditions.

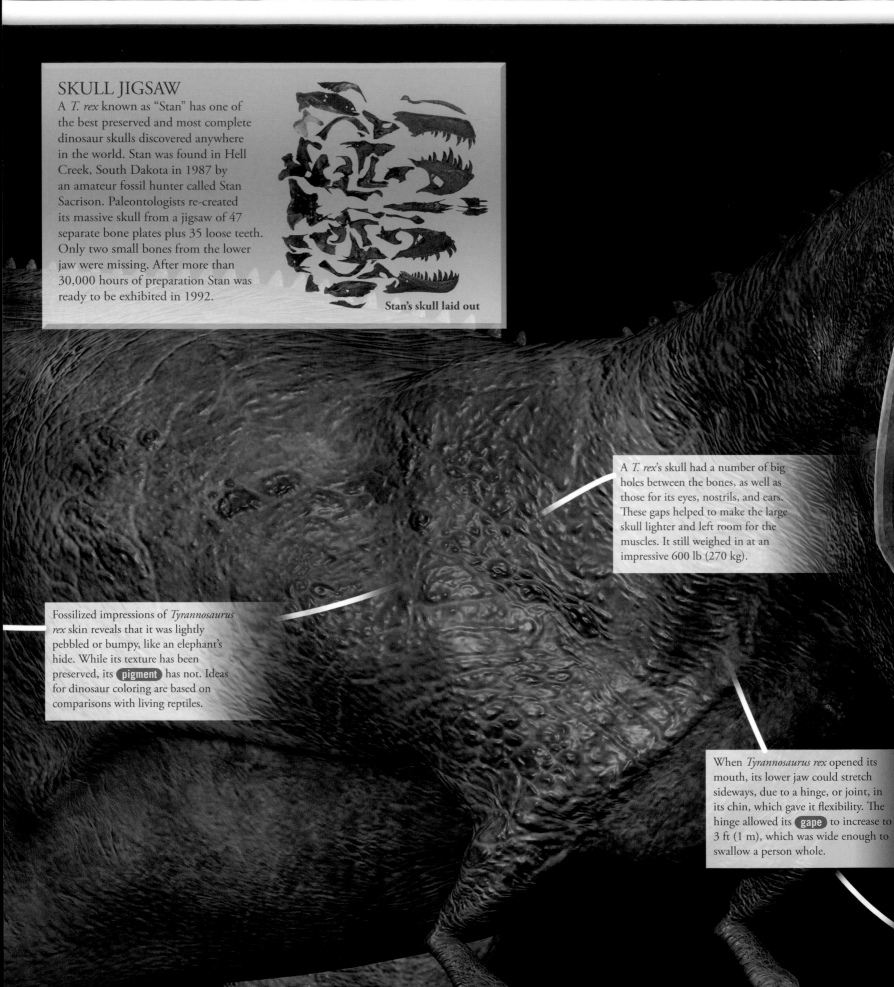

SKULL JIGSAW

A *T. rex* known as "Stan" has one of the best preserved and most complete dinosaur skulls discovered anywhere in the world. Stan was found in Hell Creek, South Dakota in 1987 by an amateur fossil hunter called Stan Sacrison. Paleontologists re-created its massive skull from a jigsaw of 47 separate bone plates plus 35 loose teeth. Only two small bones from the lower jaw were missing. After more than 30,000 hours of preparation Stan was ready to be exhibited in 1992.

Stan's skull laid out

A *T. rex*'s skull had a number of big holes between the bones, as well as those for its eyes, nostrils, and ears. These gaps helped to make the large skull lighter and left room for the muscles. It still weighed in at an impressive 600 lb (270 kg).

Fossilized impressions of *Tyrannosaurus rex* skin reveals that it was lightly pebbled or bumpy, like an elephant's hide. While its texture has been preserved, its **pigment** has not. Ideas for dinosaur coloring are based on comparisons with living reptiles.

When *Tyrannosaurus rex* opened its mouth, its lower jaw could stretch sideways, due to a hinge, or joint, in its chin, which gave it flexibility. The hinge allowed its **gape** to increase to 3 ft (1 m), which was wide enough to swallow a person whole.

pigment A substance occurring in plant or animal tissue that produces a characteristic color.

gape The extent of a widely opened verterbrate mouth.

eye sockets The two holes in a skull where the eyeballs are located.

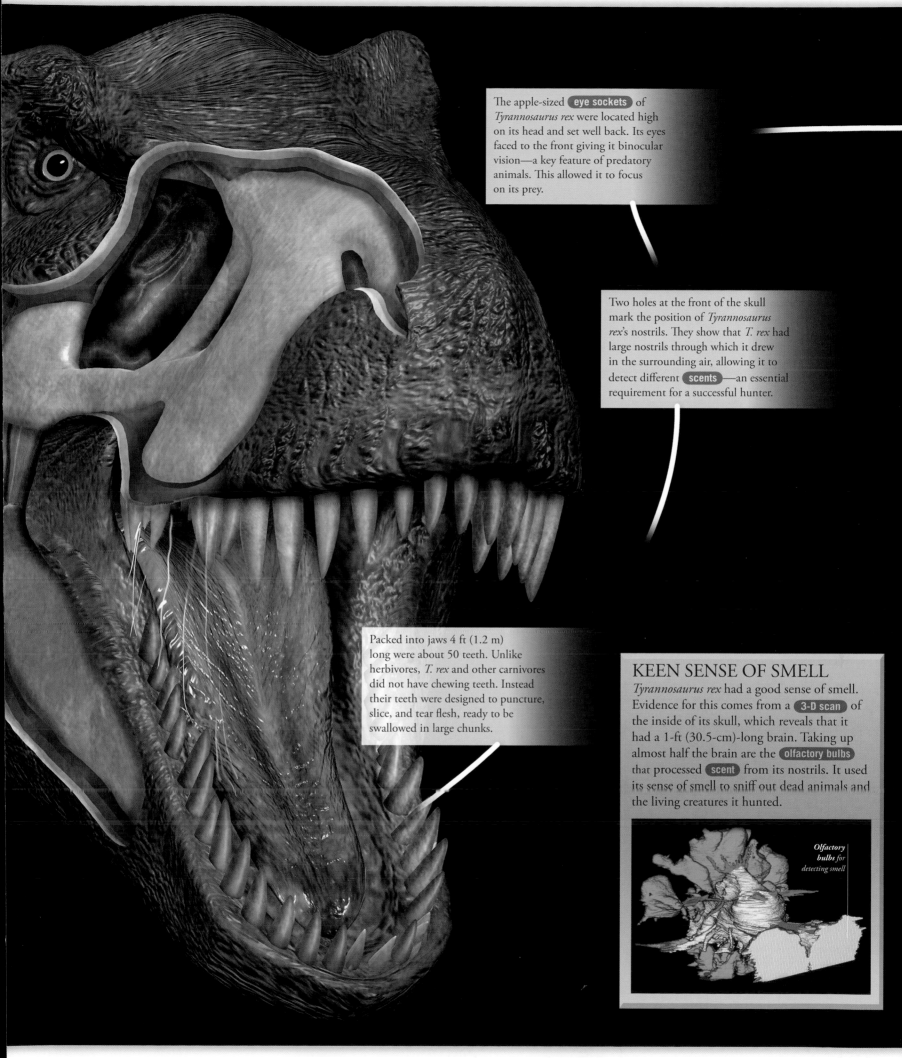

The apple-sized **eye sockets** of *Tyrannosaurus rex* were located high on its head and set well back. Its eyes faced to the front giving it binocular vision—a key feature of predatory animals. This allowed it to focus on its prey.

Two holes at the front of the skull mark the position of *Tyrannosaurus rex*'s nostrils. They show that *T. rex* had large nostrils through which it drew in the surrounding air, allowing it to detect different **scents**—an essential requirement for a successful hunter.

Packed into jaws 4 ft (1.2 m) long were about 50 teeth. Unlike herbivores, *T. rex* and other carnivores did not have chewing teeth. Instead their teeth were designed to puncture, slice, and tear flesh, ready to be swallowed in large chunks.

KEEN SENSE OF SMELL

Tyrannosaurus rex had a good sense of smell. Evidence for this comes from a **3-D scan** of the inside of its skull, which reveals that it had a 1-ft (30.5-cm)-long brain. Taking up almost half the brain are the **olfactory bulbs** that processed **scent** from its nostrils. It used its sense of smell to sniff out dead animals and the living creatures it hunted.

Olfactory bulbs for detecting smell

scent A smell left in passing, by which a human or animal may be identified.

3-D scan Computerized scanning is used to create a three-dimensional image from a series of x-rays.

olfactory bulbs The organs in the brain responsible for smell.

DISCOVERING SUE

THE MOST COMPLETE *TYRANNOSAURUS REX* EVER FOUND

S ue Hendrickson's life changed forever the day she discovered an almost complete *Tyrannosaurus rex* fossil. On August 12, 1990, Sue was with a team of professional fossil collectors near Faith, South Dakota. The small town of Faith is famous to paleontologists, as many dinosaur fossils have been excavated from bone beds nearby. On that cool, foggy morning, Sue hiked seven miles with her dog, Gypsy, to a rocky outcrop that the team had not yet investigated.

Find of a lifetime

Within minutes of reaching the outcrop, Sue knew that she had stumbled across the find of a lifetime. There were fossil bones lying at the base of the cliff, and looking up she could see larger backbones and a leg bone embedded in the side of the cliff. They were clearly from a large carnivore. Sue thought that it might be a *Tyrannosaurus rex*. She showed the bones to her colleagues, who confirmed with great excitement that they did, in fact, come from the legendary creature. The newly discovered *T. rex* was given the name "Sue" in honor of its finder.

Most complete skeleton

For 67 million years, the *Tyrannosaurus rex* had been buried deep inside its siltstone tomb, which kept its bones safe. It was this protective stone jacket that the team chipped away to reveal the dinosaur in all its glory. Over the next 17 days the team uncovered the largest and most complete *T. rex* ever found—some 200 bones in all, making up 90 percent of the dinosaur's skeleton.

Who owned Sue?

The bones were removed from the dig site and taken to a private laboratory where the long process of preparing them for display began. What should have been an enjoyable job turned into a battle over who actually owned the fossil. Did it belong to the rancher

Fossil Finder	
Name	Sue Hendrickson
Born	1949
Place of birth	Chicago, Illinois
Occupation	Paleontologist, marine archeologist

The exposed rock outcrop dates from the late Cretaceous Period. Sue Hendrickson thought that it might be a good place to look for dinosaur fossils.

"Every day we'd wake up and jokingly say, 'Today I'm gonna get me a saber-toothed cat.' But a *T. rex*? You don't even joke about that. It's too far-fetched."

Sue Hendrickson on the chances of finding a Tyrannosaurus rex.

> "She just called to me. I can't explain it but I'd never had a site draw me like that before."

Sue Hendrickson explaining why she felt drawn to the rocky outcrop.

on whose land it had been found? Did it belong to the Sioux Indian reservation that the land was part of? Did it belong to the fossil hunters because they had paid the rancher $5,000? He said that this money was for access to his land and not for the fossil. Or did it belong to the US government because it held the rancher's land in trust? These were hard questions to answer, and it took years before a court finally decided that Sue belonged to the rancher. On October 4, 1997, he sold her for a staggering world-record price of $8.4 million to The Field Museum, Chicago. In May 2000, the museum put the world's most complete *Tyrannosaurus rex* skeleton on public display.

What makes Sue special

Finding a *Tyrannosaurus rex* is rare enough but discovering one as complete as Sue is what paleontologists dream of. Now they can study the giant carnivore in great detail from head to toe. For example, before Sue, only one other *T. rex* arm had been found. Its small size had led scientists to believe that *T. rex* arms were very weak. The discovery of Sue rewrote the textbooks, for it showed that despite their size—only as long as an adult human arm—a *T.rex's* arms were incredibly strong.

Sue's snout was crushed *shortly after death. Paleontologists believe that rushing water might have flipped Sue's pelvis onto her head.*

It took 17 days to excavate *all the bones. The site was carefully mapped to record the position of each bone before it was removed.*

Sue at a Glance	
Age	Fully grown adult
Length	42 ft (12.8 m)
Height at hips	13 ft (4 m)
Live weight	6.5 tons
Skull length	5 ft (1.5 m)
Skull weight	600 lb (272 kg)
Number of teeth	58
Length of teeth	7.5–12 in (19–30 cm)
Diet	Meat
Health	Found with broken ribs, a crushed tail, and an infected jaw
Sex	Unknown, but thought to be female
Skin color	Unknown
Age at death	Thought to be old, since bones show wear and tear
Cause of death	Unknown

The skeleton's large size *provides the only clue to the dinosaur's sex. Among birds of prey—Tyrannosaurus rex's closest descendants—the females are larger than the males.*

HUNTING ITS PREY

The fossilized bones of a *Tyrannosaurus rex* once belonged to a breathing, biting, bellowing beast that roamed across the low-lying land, in what is today the state of Montana. The landscape has altered dramatically since the Cretaceous—65 million years ago, it was a patchwork of trees and swamps. Scientists can re-create its appearance by looking at rocks. Although *Tyrannosaurus rex* can be reconstructed using fossils, scientists have to look at modern hunters, such as tigers, to imagine its behavior and hunting tactics. Follow the tyrannosaur's trail as it searches for food, makes a kill, and is then forced into a showdown with another of its kind.

Weaving its way between the trunks of giant pine trees is the largest hunter ever to walk the Earth, a fully grown adult *Tyrannosaurus rex*. Despite its great size, it's a stealthy animal, and can move through the forest without drawing attention to itself.

The tyrannosaur hasn't eaten in days. Judging by lions and big meat-eaters today, it would eat a lot at one time, then not again for perhaps up to a week. Its stomach is empty, and hunger messages race along its nerves to its brain. The hunt for food begins.

Tyrannosaurus rex picks its way through the forest, its **senses** fully alert. A tyrannosaur's eyes point forward like the eyes of a lion, giving it good **depth of field** . Somewhere ahead is its unsuspecting prey, who it will detect by sight, scent, or sound.

senses Hearing, sight, smell, touch, and taste are the main senses an animal uses to experience its world.

depth of field The range an animal can see. Each eye sees a different angle and the brain combines them; it's called binocular vision.

Tyrannosaurus rex turns to face the watery sound. It knows that animals are drawn to water, gathering by rivers and pools to quench their thirst. Perhaps it will find its prey at the water's edge. Silently it sets off to investigate.

Like many other hunters, *Tyrannosaurus rex* has a very good sense of smell. It opens its nostrils wide and sniffs hard, taking in a lungful of air. The scents of the forest are blasted along its **nasal passages**.

Every so often *Tyrannosaurus rex* stops and listens, tilting its head from side to side. The sounds of the forest flood into its ears—branches creaking, flying insects buzzing, and nearby the sound of something moving through water.

The air is filled with many mixed scents. Instantly, the tyrannosaur's brain identifies them. It detects the sweet smell of pine **resin**, the rotten smell of old dung, and the unmistakable scent of food. Mealtime is fast approaching.

nasal passages Airways along which air passes when it is inhaled. Nerve endings there send signals to the brain to help detect smells.

resin A sticky, gumlike substance produced by trees, especially conifers such as pine. Fossils have been found in hardened resin.

33

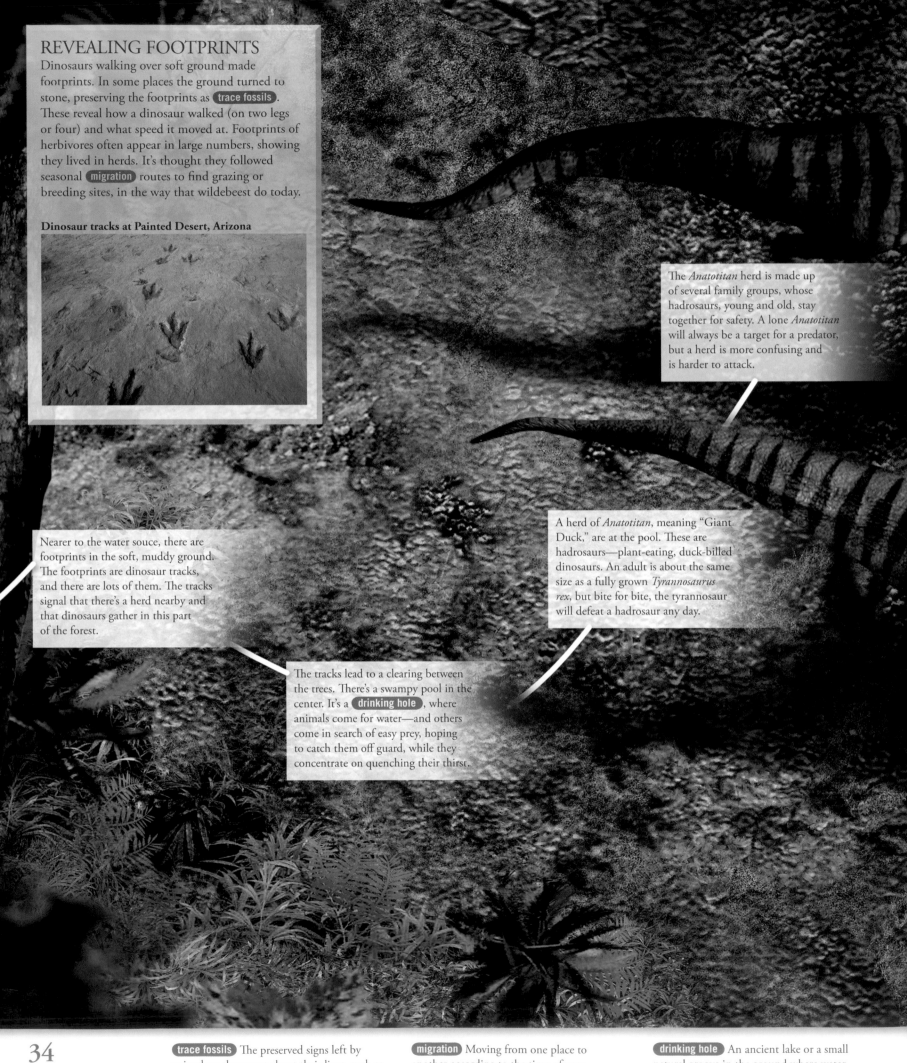

REVEALING FOOTPRINTS

Dinosaurs walking over soft ground made footprints. In some places the ground turned to stone, preserving the footprints as trace fossils. These reveal how a dinosaur walked (on two legs or four) and what speed it moved at. Footprints of herbivores often appear in large numbers, showing they lived in herds. It's thought they followed seasonal migration routes to find grazing or breeding sites, in the way that wildebeest do today.

Dinosaur tracks at Painted Desert, Arizona

The *Anatotitan* herd is made up of several family groups, whose hadrosaurs, young and old, stay together for safety. A lone *Anatotitan* will always be a target for a predator, but a herd is more confusing and is harder to attack.

Nearer to the water souce, there are footprints in the soft, muddy ground. The footprints are dinosaur tracks, and there are lots of them. The tracks signal that there's a herd nearby and that dinosaurs gather in this part of the forest.

A herd of *Anatotitan*, meaning "Giant Duck," are at the pool. These are hadrosaurs—plant-eating, duck-billed dinosaurs. An adult is about the same size as a fully grown *Tyrannosaurus rex*, but bite for bite, the tyrannosaur will defeat a hadrosaur any day.

The tracks lead to a clearing between the trees. There's a swampy pool in the center. It's a drinking hole, where animals come for water—and others come in search of easy prey, hoping to catch them off guard, while they concentrate on quenching their thirst.

trace fossils The preserved signs left by animals as they went about their lives, such as tracks, footprints, eggs, nests, and droppings.

migration Moving from one place to another according to the time of year.

drinking hole An ancient lake or a small natural groove in the ground where water collects and animals gather to drink.

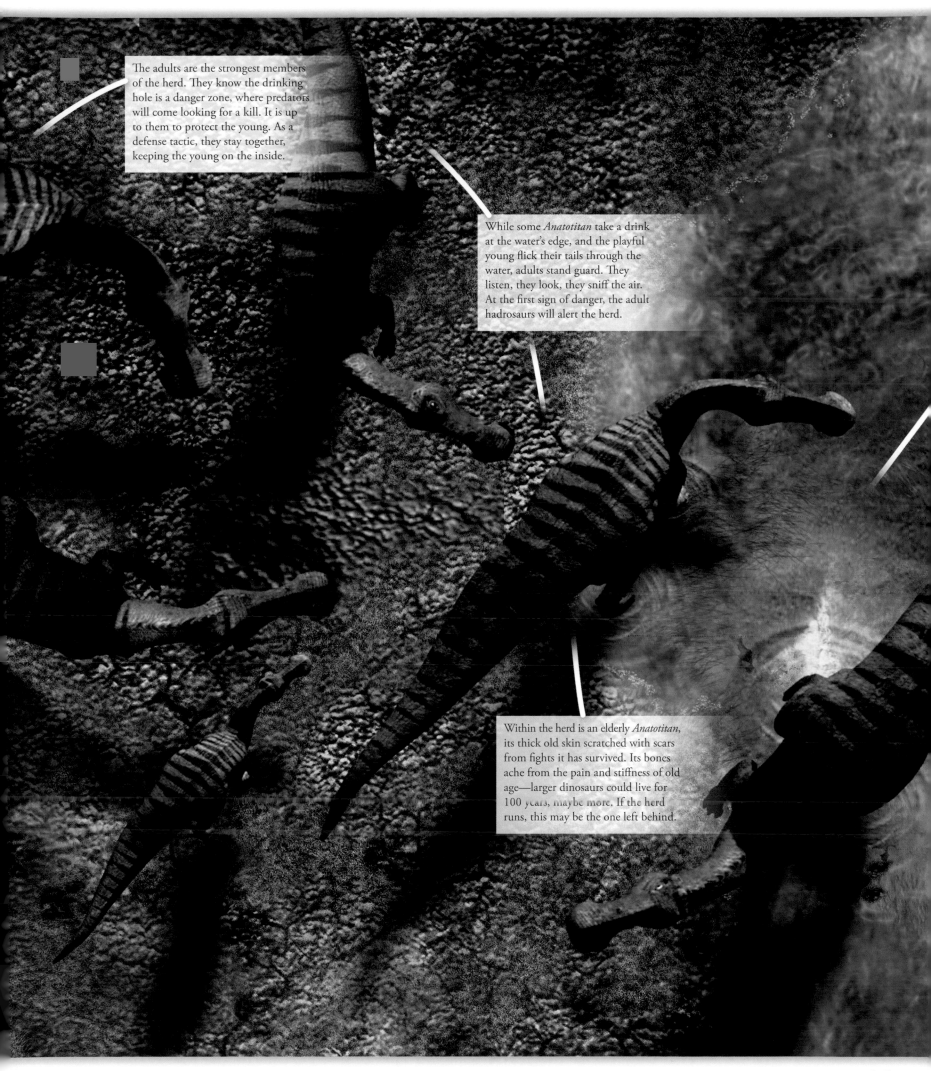

The adults are the strongest members of the herd. They know the drinking hole is a danger zone, where predators will come looking for a kill. It is up to them to protect the young. As a defense tactic, they stay together, keeping the young on the inside.

While some *Anatotitan* take a drink at the water's edge, and the playful young flick their tails through the water, adults stand guard. They listen, they look, they sniff the air. At the first sign of danger, the adult hadrosaurs will alert the herd.

Within the herd is an elderly *Anatotitan*, its thick old skin scratched with scars from fights it has survived. Its bones ache from the pain and stiffness of old age—larger dinosaurs could live for 100 years, maybe more. If the herd runs, this may be the one left behind.

Alerted by a noise, the herd of *Anatotitan* stops feeding and they raise their heads. The fearful scent of the *Tyrannosaurus rex* fills their nostrils. The hunter has outsmarted them by approaching into the wind so they have not detected its scent until now.

Anatotitan are herd-dwellers, so they act as one. When one panics, they all panic. The first to move sets them off, scattering in every direction. This is a defense mechanism, confusing a predator and making it harder for it to single out one animal.

The giant duck-bills call out, their cries of alarm amplified by enlarged nasal passages, alerting all to the danger. They signal their distress in other ways, too. **Sacs** of skin inflate from their snouts, flushed with color, like blood-red balloons.

TYRANNOSAURUS MEALS

Tyrannosaurus rex's giant size was matched by an enormous appetite, and the bigger the kill, the less hunting it had to do. Its size, strength, and fearsome teeth made it powerful enough to attack other giants of the Cretaceous Period, including hadrosaurs, such as *Anatotitan* and *Edmontosaurus,* as well as the heavily armored *Triceratops* and *Euoplocephalus*. Other sources of food probably included carrion, the decaying flesh of dead animals. In these cases, *Tyrannosaurus rex* acted as a **scavenger**, not a hunter. If it came across an animal that was already dead, perhaps it died of natural causes or was killed by another animal, then it might have had a free lunch without having to hunt.

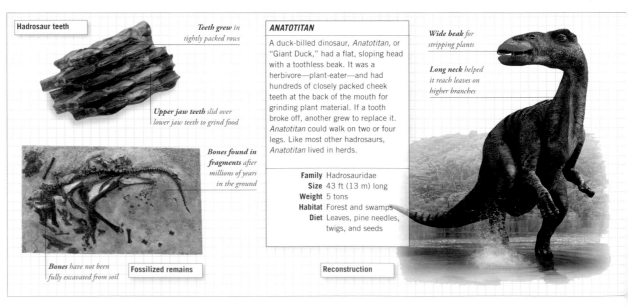

Hadrosaur teeth

Teeth grew in tightly packed rows

Upper jaw teeth slid over lower jaw teeth to grind food

Bones found in fragments after millions of years in the ground

Bones have not been fully excavated from soil **Fossilized remains**

ANATOTITAN

A duck-billed dinosaur, *Anatotitan*, or "Giant Duck," had a flat, sloping head with a toothless beak. It was a herbivore—plant-eater—and had hundreds of closely packed cheek teeth at the back of the mouth for grinding plant material. If a tooth broke off, another grew to replace it. *Anatotitan* could walk on two or four legs. Like most other hadrosaurs, *Anatotitan* lived in herds.

Family	Hadrosauridae
Size	43 ft (13 m) long
Weight	5 tons
Habitat	Forest and swamps
Diet	Leaves, pine needles, twigs, and seeds

Reconstruction

Wide beak for stripping plants

Long neck helped it reach leaves on higher branches

scavenger An animal that searches for and eats meat from animals that they did not kill themselves.

sacs Bags of skin that can be inflated, or blown up, to increase the sound of their calls, similar to the vocal sacs of male frogs.

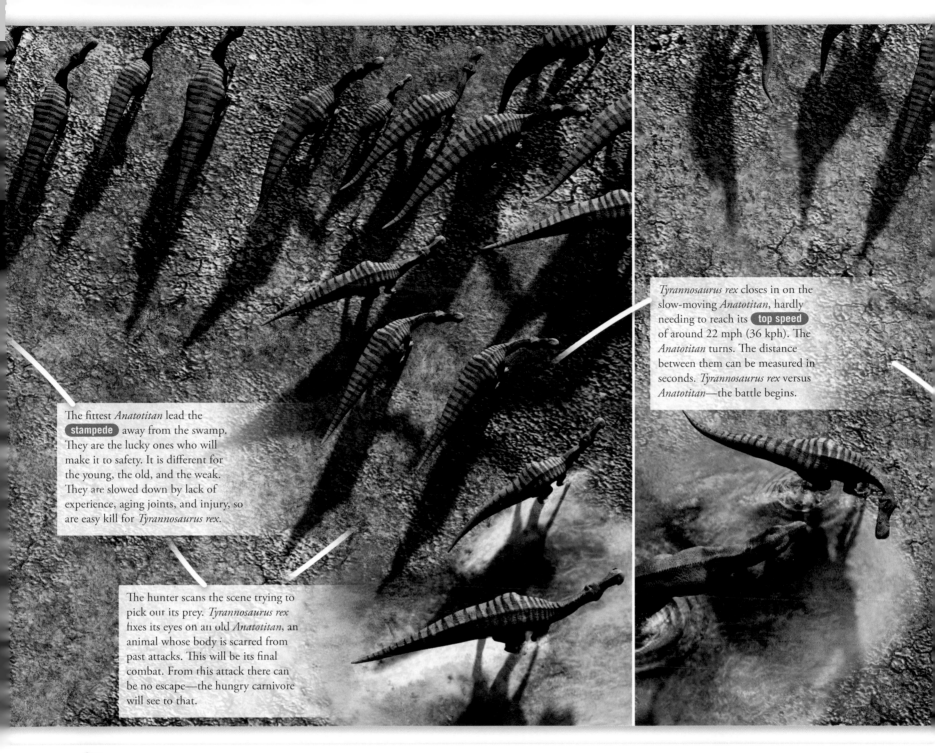

Tyrannosaurus rex closes in on the slow-moving *Anatotitan*, hardly needing to reach its `top speed` of around 22 mph (36 kph). The *Anatotitan* turns. The distance between them can be measured in seconds. *Tyrannosaurus rex* versus *Anatotitan*—the battle begins.

The fittest *Anatotitan* lead the `stampede` away from the swamp. They are the lucky ones who will make it to safety. It is different for the young, the old, and the weak. They are slowed down by lack of experience, aging joints, and injury, so are easy kill for *Tyrannosaurus rex*.

The hunter scans the scene trying to pick out its prey. *Tyrannosaurus rex* fixes its eyes on an old *Anatotitan*, an animal whose body is scarred from past attacks. This will be its final combat. From this attack there can be no escape—the hungry carnivore will see to that.

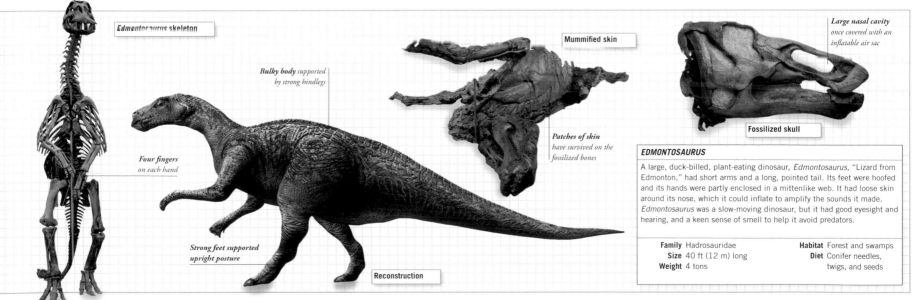

Edmontosaurus skeleton

Bulky body *supported by strong hindlegs*

Four fingers *on each hand*

Strong feet supported *upright posture*

Reconstruction

Mummified skin

Patches of skin *have survived on the fossilized bones*

Large nasal cavity *once covered with an inflatable air sac*

Fossilized skull

EDMONTOSAURUS

A large, duck-billed, plant-eating dinosaur, *Edmontosaurus*, "Lizard from Edmonton," had short arms and a long, pointed tail. Its feet were hoofed and its hands were partly enclosed in a mittenlike web. It had loose skin around its nose, which it could inflate to amplify the sounds it made. *Edmontosaurus* was a slow-moving dinosaur, but it had good eyesight and hearing, and a keen sense of smell to help it avoid predators.

Family	Hadrosauridae	**Habitat**	Forest and swamps
Size	40 ft (12 m) long	**Diet**	Conifer needles,
Weight	4 tons		twigs, and seeds

`stampede` When a group of animals rushes in the same direction at the same time.

`top speed` *Tyrannosaurus rex*'s fastest pace—estimates are based on its leg size, and comparisons with modern animals.

`mummified` Shriveled and dried up body parts that have been preserved.

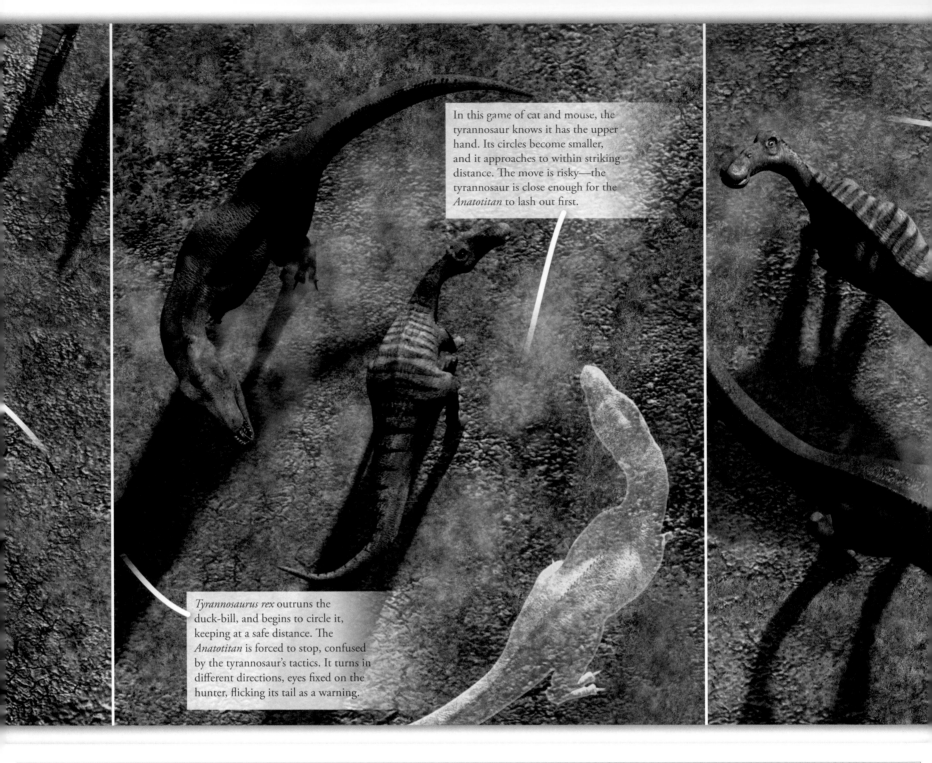

In this game of cat and mouse, the tyrannosaur knows it has the upper hand. Its circles become smaller, and it approaches to within striking distance. The move is risky—the tyrannosaur is close enough for the *Anatotitan* to lash out first.

Tyrannosaurus rex outruns the duck-bill, and begins to circle it, keeping at a safe distance. The *Anatotitan* is forced to stop, confused by the tyrannosaur's tactics. It turns in different directions, eyes fixed on the hunter, flicking its tail as a warning.

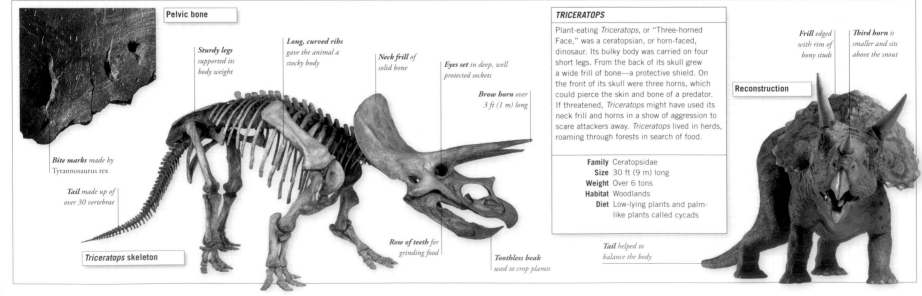

Pelvic bone

Sturdy legs *supported its body weight*

Long, curved ribs *gave the animal a stocky body*

Neck frill *of solid bone*

Eyes set *in deep, well protected sockets*

Brow horn *over 3 ft (1 m) long*

Bite marks *made by* Tyrannosaurus rex

Tail *made up of over 30 vertebrae*

Triceratops skeleton

Row of teeth *for grinding food*

Toothless beak *used to crop plants*

TRICERATOPS

Plant-eating *Triceratops*, or "Three-horned Face," was a ceratopsian, or horn-faced, dinosaur. Its bulky body was carried on four short legs. From the back of its skull grew a wide frill of bone—a protective shield. On the front of its skull were three horns, which could pierce the skin and bone of a predator. If threatened, *Triceratops* might have used its neck frill and horns in a show of aggression to scare attackers away. *Triceratops* lived in herds, roaming through forests in search of food.

Family	Ceratopsidae
Size	30 ft (9 m) long
Weight	Over 6 tons
Habitat	Woodlands
Diet	Low-lying plants and palm-like plants called cycads

Frill *edged with rim of bony studs*

Third horn *is smaller and sits above the snout*

Reconstruction

Tail *helped to balance the body*

38

With a flick of its tail, the *Anatotitan* connects with the tyrannosaur, striking its body with force. *Tyrannosaurus rex* backs off. If the *Anatotitan* had struck lower, it could have broken the tyrannosaur's leg, and felled its pursuer.

Seizing the moment, the *Anatotitan* makes a run for it, heading toward the cover of the forest. But it makes slow progress. With so much ground between it and safety, the faster *Tyrannosaurus rex* will soon catch up with it.

Chasing after the *Anatotitan*, *Tyrannosaurus* comes up fast on its inside. The *Anatotitan's* tail is no threat this time. All of the hadrosaur's energy is focused into running away, in a desperate bid to reach safety, but the hadrosaur is tiring fast.

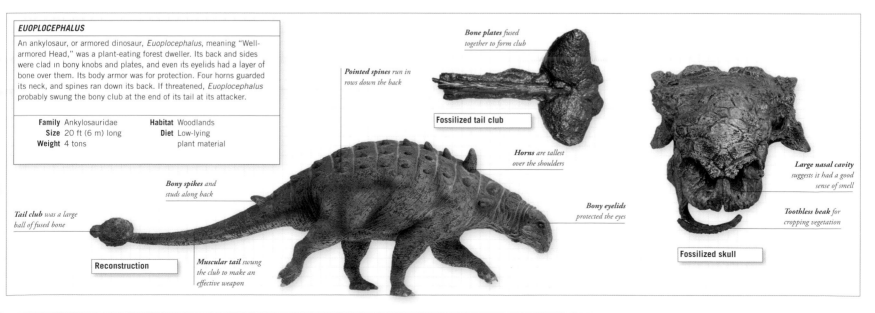

EUOPLOCEPHALUS

An ankylosaur, or armored dinosaur, *Euoplocephalus*, meaning "Well-armored Head," was a plant-eating forest dweller. Its back and sides were clad in bony knobs and plates, and even its eyelids had a layer of bone over them. Its body armor was for protection. Four horns guarded its neck, and spines ran down its back. If threatened, *Euoplocephalus* probably swung the bony club at the end of its tail at its attacker.

Family	Ankylosauridae	**Habitat**	Woodlands
Size	20 ft (6 m) long	**Diet**	Low-lying
Weight	4 tons		plant material

Bone plates *fused together to form club*

Pointed spines *run in rows down the back*

Fossilized tail club

Horns *are tallest over the shoulders*

Large nasal cavity *suggests it had a good sense of smell*

Bony spikes *and studs along back*

Bony eyelids *protected the eyes*

Tail club *was a large ball of fused bone*

Toothless beak *for cropping vegetation*

Reconstruction

Muscular tail *swung the club to make an effective weapon*

Fossilized skull

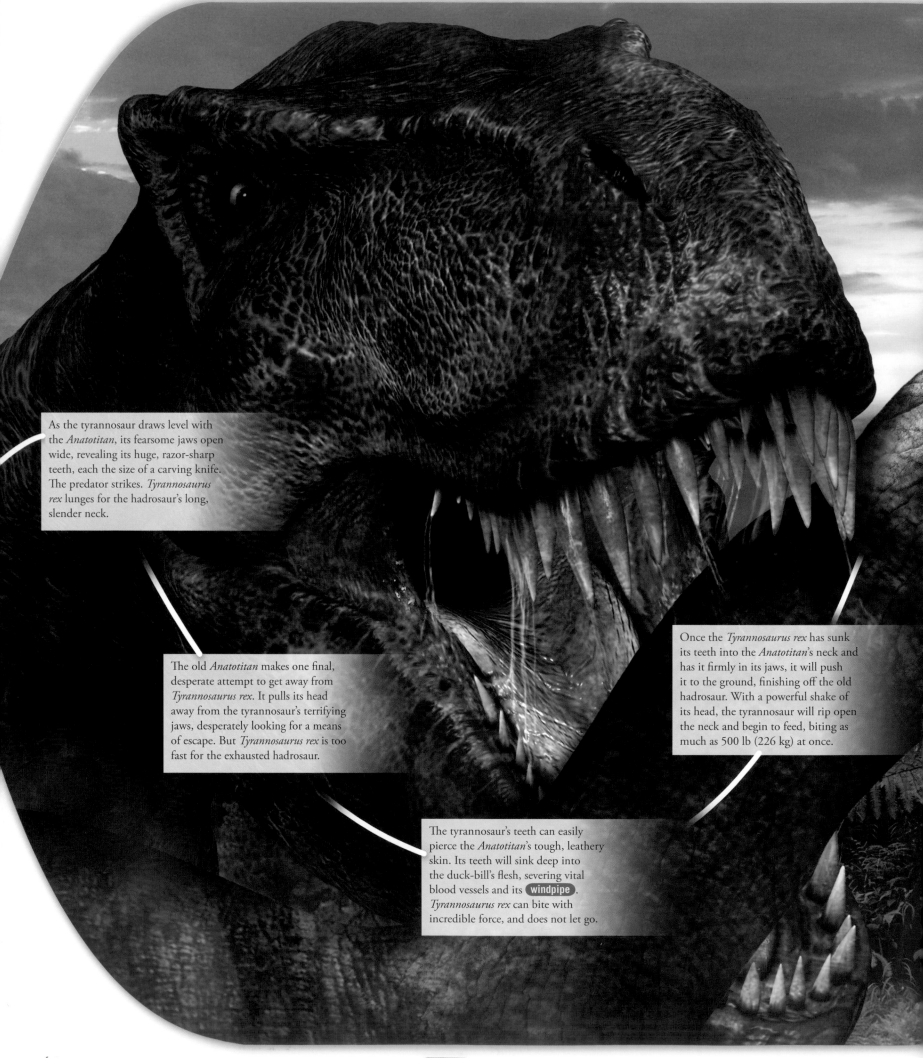

As the tyrannosaur draws level with the *Anatotitan*, its fearsome jaws open wide, revealing its huge, razor-sharp teeth, each the size of a carving knife. The predator strikes. *Tyrannosaurus rex* lunges for the hadrosaur's long, slender neck.

The old *Anatotitan* makes one final, desperate attempt to get away from *Tyrannosaurus rex*. It pulls its head away from the tyrannosaur's terrifying jaws, desperately looking for a means of escape. But *Tyrannosaurus rex* is too fast for the exhausted hadrosaur.

Once the *Tyrannosaurus rex* has sunk its teeth into the *Anatotitan*'s neck and has it firmly in its jaws, it will push it to the ground, finishing off the old hadrosaur. With a powerful shake of its head, the tyrannosaur will rip open the neck and begin to feed, biting as much as 500 lb (226 kg) at once.

The tyrannosaur's teeth can easily pierce the *Anatotitan*'s tough, leathery skin. Its teeth will sink deep into the duck-bill's flesh, severing vital blood vessels and its windpipe . *Tyrannosaurus rex* can bite with incredible force, and does not let go.

windpipe The airway that leads from the throat to the lungs.

The predator has not eaten for several days, so it will gorge itself on its kill. Using its tiny arms to pin the *Anatotitan*'s corpse to the ground, its jaws can close in on the soft flesh of the belly, then it pulls hard to tear off a mouthful of food.

Tyrannosaurus rex did not chew its food in the way that humans do, as its upper and lower teeth did not meet together. It did not crunch the bones, but the force of its bite would have broken the bones that eventually pass out, undigested, in its dung.

The dead *Anatotitan* is a meal to be enjoyed over several days, not rushed all at once. The tyrannosaur will stay in the area, returning to feed on its kill, which it will have to guard from scavengers looking for a ready meal.

PUNCTURE AND PULL

Death came quickly to an animal bitten by *Tyrannosaurus rex*. It inflicted massive injuries with its powerful jaws and sharp, pointed teeth. To feed off its victim's flesh, it used a technique know as "puncture and pull." The tyrannosaur bit into the body of its prey, sinking its teeth as deep as they would go. With its jaws tightly clamped, it jerked its head from side to side, tugging hard while moving backward. The victim's skin and flesh ripped open, and the tyrannosaur pulled off a bite-sized chunk of meat. Scientists worked out the gruesome technique by studying the positions and shapes of 80 *Tyrannosaurus rex* teeth marks found in a *Triceratops'* pelvis .

TYRANNOSAURUS REX TOOTH

Serrated edge to slice through flesh

Front teeth could be 12 in (30 cm) long

pelvis Basin-shaped bone at the base of the spine that supports the back limbs.

41

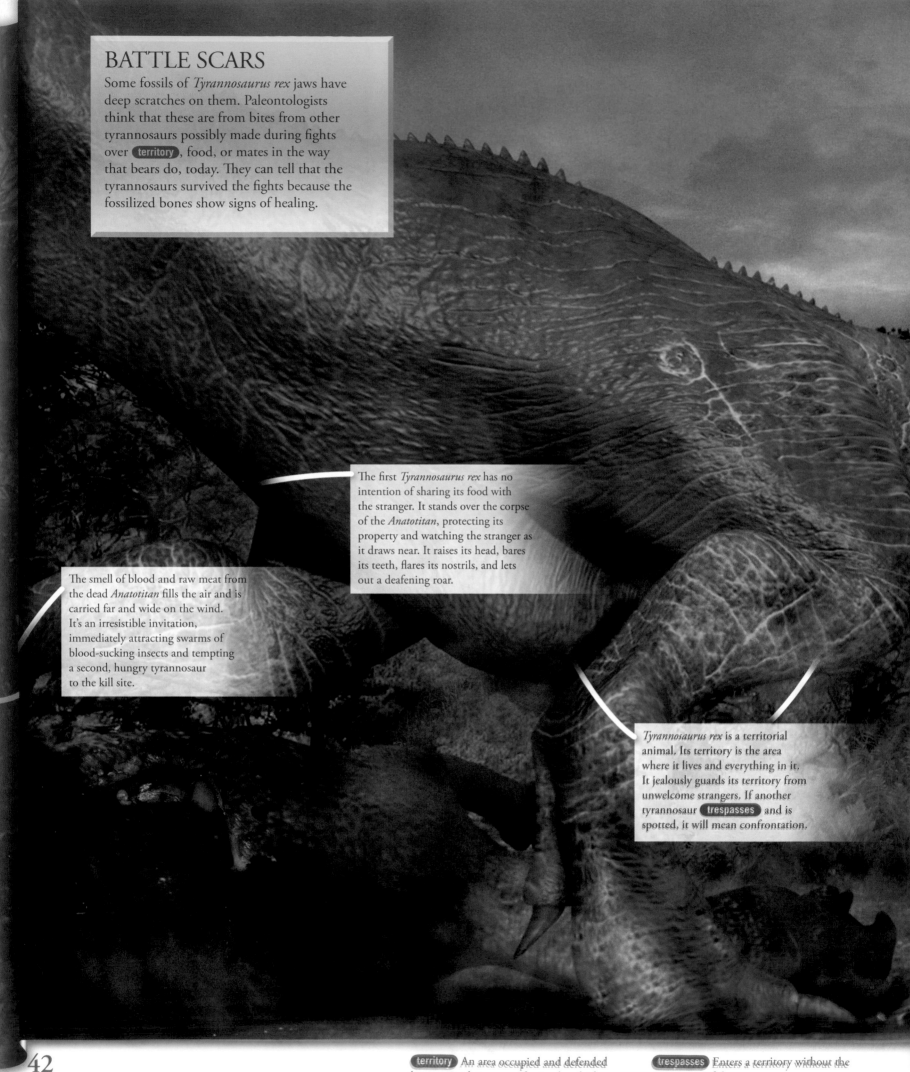

BATTLE SCARS

Some fossils of *Tyrannosaurus rex* jaws have deep scratches on them. Paleontologists think that these are from bites from other tyrannosaurs possibly made during fights over **territory**, food, or mates in the way that bears do, today. They can tell that the tyrannosaurs survived the fights because the fossilized bones show signs of healing.

The first *Tyrannosaurus rex* has no intention of sharing its food with the stranger. It stands over the corpse of the *Anatotitan*, protecting its property and watching the stranger as it draws near. It raises its head, bares its teeth, flares its nostrils, and lets out a deafening roar.

The smell of blood and raw meat from the dead *Anatotitan* fills the air and is carried far and wide on the wind. It's an irresistible invitation, immediately attracting swarms of blood-sucking insects and tempting a second, hungry tyrannosaur to the kill site.

Tyrannosaurus rex is a territorial animal. Its territory is the area where it lives and everything in it. It jealously guards its territory from unwelcome strangers. If another tyrannosaur **trespasses** and is spotted, it will mean confrontation.

territory An area occupied and defended by an animal or group of animals, which includes their feeding and breeding grounds.

trespasses Enters a territory without the permission of the owner.

The two tyrannosaurs come head to head – eyes staring, snouts almost touching, tails flicking from side to side. It begins as a **stand-off** to see which of them can out-stare the other. But when one nudges the other with his snout, the contest moves into a more violent phase.

The tyrannosaurs tilt their heads sideways and try to bite each other's jaws, looking for the best angle for attack. The first *Tyrannosaurus rex* strikes, biting the stranger's upper jaw and crunching down hard on it. It doesn't let go, even though a tooth snaps off.

The stranger knows it cannot win. Rather than risk greater injury, it stops struggling. It submits to the stronger tyrannosaur, who relaxes its grip and sets the stranger free. The second tyrannosaur backs away, its head bowed low in defeat. It must look elsewhere for food.

The first *Tyrannosaurus rex* has won the contest and gets back to its feast. Seeing the tyrannosaurs fight, a small, plant-eating *Leptoceratops,* or "Slender Horn Face," scrurries away. It does not want to become the next victim of a hungry *Tyrannosaurus rex*.

stand-off Stalemate or deadlock between opponents in which no progress can be made or any agreement reached.

CARNIVORES CATALOG

Paleontologists describe all carnivorous or meat-eating dinosaurs as theropods, meaning "beast-footed." *T. rex* is probably the best known of these bipedal or two-footed creatures with their birdlike bodies, sharp teeth and claws, and long tails. But theropods came in all sizes, and for millions of years they were the world's main predators, hunting or scavenging, alone or in packs. Their fossilized remains have been found throughout the world.

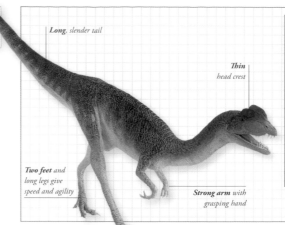

Long, slender tail

Thin head crest

Two feet and long legs give speed and agility

Strong arm with grasping hand

DILOPHOSAURUS

The largest meat-eater of the early Jurassic Period, *Dilophosaurus* was probably a fast and agile hunter. It had two bony crests on its head which may have been used during courtship displays, perhaps changing color to attract a mate.

Name means	"Two-Crested Lizard"
Time	Early Jurassic (190 mya)
Size	19 ft 6 in (6 m) long
Where found	North America, China
Habitat	Scrub and woodland
Diet	Small animals, fish

ALLOSAURUS

Allosaurus was the first of the giant meat-eaters. Its curved teeth were serrated like a steak knife in order to slice through meat, while its strong claws were used to grip its prey. Footprint evidence shows that it hunted in packs.

Name means	"Other Lizard"
Time	Late Jurassic (150 mya)
Size	39 ft (12 m) long
Where found	North America
Habitat	Open countryside
Diet	Herbivores

Allosaurus skull

Long tail balances body

Claws up to 10 in (25 cm) long

Sharp teeth point backwards

Leg powered by strong muscles

Long, slender neck

Flexible tail

Grasping, clawed hand

Legs are long and birdlike

COELOPHYSIS

One of the first meat-eating dinosaurs, *Coelophysis* was probably a pack animal that hunted for small prey in a group. It was also a cannibal—crushed bones from other *Coelophysis* have been found inside its fossilized stomach area.

Name means	"Hollow Form"
Time	Late Triassic (220 mya)
Size	10 ft (3 m) long
Where found	North America
Habitat	Semidesert terrain
Diet	Lizards, fish

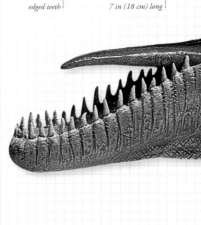

Bladelike, saw-edged teeth

Each tooth 7 in (18 cm) long

COMPSOGNATHUS

Compsognathus was one of the smallest dinosaurs and was no bigger than a cat. Its compact body and long, slender legs show that it was built for speed. Its jaws had small, sharp teeth and it probably hunted small lizards and large insects.

Name means	"Pretty Jaw"
Time	Late Jurassic (145 mya)
Size	3 ft (1 m) long
Where found	Europe
Habitat	Semidesert terrain
Diet	Lizards

Large eye to spot prey

Skin covered with scales

Long, whiplike tail

Sharp, curved teeth

Three-toed clawed foot

Two clawed fingers

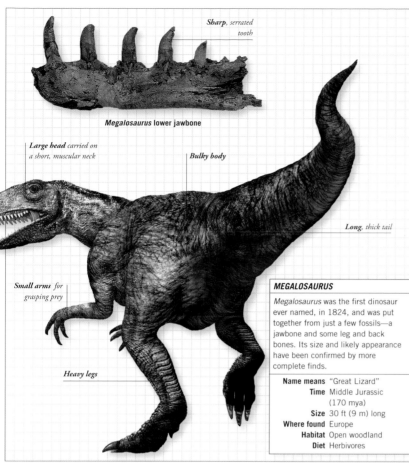

Sharp, serrated tooth

Megalosaurus lower jawbone

Large head carried on a short, muscular neck

Bulky body

Long, thick tail

Small arms for grasping prey

Heavy legs

MEGALOSAURUS

Megalosaurus was the first dinosaur ever named, in 1824, and was put together from just a few fossils—a jawbone and some leg and back bones. Its size and likely appearance have been confirmed by more complete finds.

Name means	"Great Lizard"
Time	Middle Jurassic (170 mya)
Size	30 ft (9 m) long
Where found	Europe
Habitat	Open woodland
Diet	Herbivores

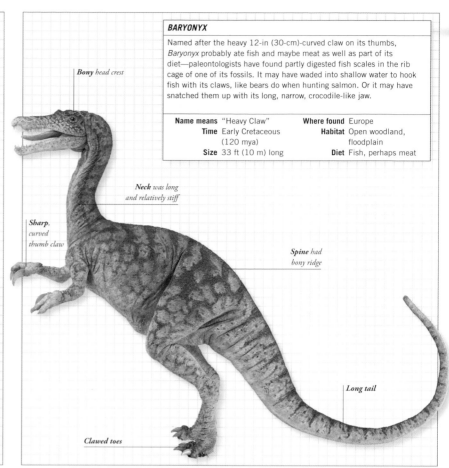

BARYONYX

Named after the heavy 12-in (30-cm)-curved claw on its thumbs, *Baryonyx* probably ate fish and maybe meat as well as part of its diet—paleontologists have found partly digested fish scales in the rib cage of one of its fossils. It may have waded into shallow water to hook fish with its claws, like bears do when hunting salmon. Or it may have snatched them up with its long, narrow, crocodile-like jaw.

Name means	"Heavy Claw"	**Where found**	Europe
Time	Early Cretaceous (120 mya)	**Habitat**	Open woodland, floodplain
Size	33 ft (10 m) long	**Diet**	Fish, perhaps meat

Bony head crest

Neck was long and relatively stiff

Sharp, curved thumb claw

Spine had bony ridge

Long tail

Clawed toes

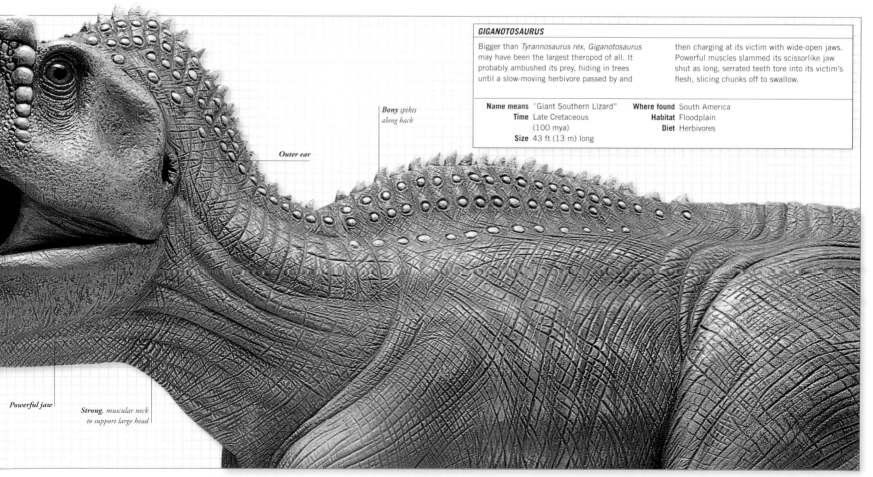

GIGANOTOSAURUS

Bigger than *Tyrannosaurus rex*, *Giganotosaurus* may have been the largest theropod of all. It probably ambushed its prey, hiding in trees until a slow-moving herbivore passed by and then charging at its victim with wide-open jaws. Powerful muscles slammed its scissorlike jaw shut as long, serrated teeth tore into its victim's flesh, slicing chunks off to swallow.

Name means	"Giant Southern Lizard"	**Where found**	South America
Time	Late Cretaceous (100 mya)	**Habitat**	Floodplain
Size	43 ft (13 m) long	**Diet**	Herbivores

Bony spikes along back

Outer ear

Powerful jaw

Strong, muscular neck to support large head

METEORITE STRIKE

HOW A GIANT ROCK CAUSED MASS EXTINCTION

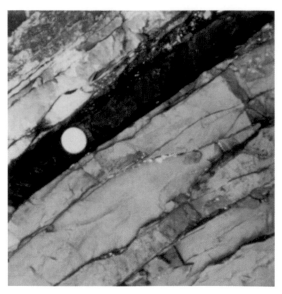

A coin shows the thin clay K-T layer that marks the boundary between Cretaceous and Tertiary rock. The clay contains iridium, a metal found in meteorites.

Sixty-five million years ago the dinosaurs died out. Why? Dozens of extinction theories have been put forward to explain how they were wiped out, but by the 1980s one theory was being taken more seriously than any other. Maybe a meteorite—a giant lump of rock from space—had smashed into the Earth, causing dramatic climate change and the mass extinction of the dinosaurs. Coming up with the idea was one thing, proving it was something else.

Forams are tiny, single-celled organisms that died out at the same time as the dinosaurs.

Examining fossils

The meteorite impact theory was first proposed by Dr. Walter Alvarez, a geologist from the University of California, in 1980. He had been working near Gubbio in central Italy, collecting samples of microscopic fossils called foraminiferans (commonly shortened to forams) from the local limestone rocks. Limestone is made from the fossilized shells of dead sea creatures that collect on the shallow ocean floor. As layers of sediment built up over millions of years, immense pressure squeezed the water out and cemented the sediment together to form solid limestone and chalk (a softer limestone). Many of the original shells were preserved in this rock. While studying these fossilized forams, Alvarez made an unexpected discovery.

The K-T boundary

Alvarez found that there were two distinct ages of rock at Gubbio. The oldest rocks dated from the Cretaceous Period, when dinosaurs still roamed the Earth. The youngest rocks dated from the Tertiary Period, after the dinosaurs had become extinct. In between these two layers was a thin band of clay. Scientists now refer to this dividing layer as the K-T boundary, since it marks the end of the Cretaceous Period (K—from *kreta,* the Greek word for chalk—to avoid confusion with the earlier Cambrian and Carboniferous Periods) and the start of the Tertiary Period (T). Alvarez

noticed that there were many forams in the Cretaceous and Tertiary rocks but very few in the clay layer that had formed between these rocks. He wondered what had caused the foram population to virtually disappear at the end of the Cretaceous Period. Could the same destructive force also be responsible for the extinction of the dinosaurs? Alvarez wondered if the answers lay inside the mysterious layer of clay.

Secret in the clay

In the laboratory, Walter Alvarez worked with his father, Professor Luis Alvarez, to find out how long it had taken for the layer of clay at Gubbio to form. Was it tens, thousands, or millions of years? The answer would show how long it had taken for the foram population to decline at the end of the Cretaceous Period. Since their mass death

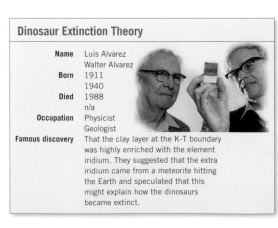

Dinosaur Extinction Theory	
Name	Luis Alvarez Walter Alvarez
Born	1911 1940
Died	1988 n/a
Occupation	Physicist Geologist
Famous discovery	That the clay layer at the K-T boundary was highly enriched with the element iridium. They suggested that the extra iridium came from a meteorite hitting the Earth and speculated that this might explain how the dinosaurs became extinct.

coincided with the end of the dinosaurs, it would be possible to see if the dinosaurs had died out slowly, over a long period, or suddenly, over a short period.

Metal detector

To find the answer, Luis Alvarez, a physicist, measured how much iridium there was in the Gubbio clay. He knew that this rare metal came from space dust that fell on the planet at a known, steady rate. Once he had worked out how much iridium was in the clay, he could say how long it had taken to form. He discovered that there was a lot more than he had expected to find. Luis and Walter then checked the iridium levels in the rocks above and below the clay layer but found them to be normal. There was only one explanation for this anomaly—an extraterrestrial object must have dumped the extra iridium on the Earth's surface.

Meteorite hits the Earth

In 1980, Luis and Walter Alvarez announced their discovery and suggested that this iridium had been brought to Earth by a giant meteorite. It would have vaporized on impact, releasing iridium dust into the atmosphere, which then settled around the world. Walter had detected the iridium in Italy;

The **Chicxulub impact crater**, found at the top of the Yucatán peninsula in Mexico, was caused by a meteorite 6–9 mile (10–14 km) wide hitting the Earth around 65 mya.

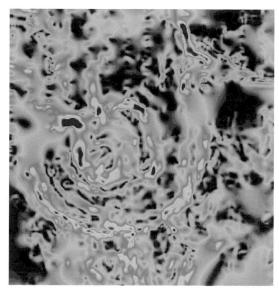

This gravity map shows the extent of the Chicxulub crater. The larger green, yellow, and red semicircle shows the crater rim on the land.

other scientists were finding it elsewhere. To back up their theory, they needed to find an impact crater of the right size and the right age.

Finding the crater

In 1978, two years before Luis and Walter Alvarez proposed their meteorite impact theory, Glen Penfield, a geophysicist, was surveying the Gulf of Mexico just off the Yucatán peninsula for an oil company. As he mapped his data, he noticed an unexpected arc shape deep underground. Intrigued, Penfield matched an earlier gravity chart to his own and saw that this arc formed part of a huge circle about 112 miles (180 km)

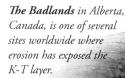

*The **Badlands** in Alberta, Canada, is one of several sites worldwide where erosion has exposed the K-T layer.*

wide, with its epicenter in the village of Chicxulub. Penfield realized that the circle was the rim of a giant crater caused by a meteorite hitting the Earth. He announced his discovery in 1981 but his report attracted little attention at the time. It took another 10 years for someone to build on his findings. In 1990, Alan Hildebrand, from the University of Arizona, reported glassy fragments and high levels of iridium on the Caribbean island of Haiti. He was sure that they must have been caused by an ancient meteorite impact in the region. When a reporter told him about the Chicxulub Crater, he knew that he had found their source. The Chicxulub iridium was dated to 65 million years and linked with the iridium that Alvarez had found in Gubbio.

Death from the sky

The Chicxulub Crater provided proof that a giant meteorite had collided with the Earth 65 million years ago, causing devastation on a global scale. There would have been earthquakes and tsunamis, and a huge volume of dust would have been thrown up into the atmosphere. As the dust covered the planet, temperatures would have fallen and sunlight would have been reduced. Without warmth and daylight to sustain them, around 85 percent of plants and animals—from forams to dinosaurs—would have died, probably within a few weeks.

EXTINCTION!

At the end of the Cretaceous Period, Earth had a visitor from space. It was a large **meteorite**—a vast rock that came without warning, smashed into the planet, and caused a global catastrophe. Huge numbers of plants and animals died out in the chaos that followed. Fifty percent of all living creatures became **extinct**. Earth had suffered from mass extinction events before, such as at the end of the Permian (251 mya) when many marine animals and reptiles died out. But on this occasion the impact changed the course of life on Earth. The event destroyed the world of the dinosaurs, and after ruling for 185 million years they were gone, leaving other groups of animals to inherit the planet.

The force from the impact is as great as the explosion from 100 million **megatons** of explosive. A crater some 112 miles (180 km) across and 10 miles (15 km) deep is punched into the planet's crust, causing rings of mountains to form at its rim.

The speeding meteorite strikes Earth at an angle of 45 degrees, plunging into a shallow sea. The impact site is a coastal zone of coral reefs in what is today the Gulf of Mexico, between the continents of North and South America.

As the meteorite enters Earth's atmosphere, it feels the effects of **friction** on its surface. It heats up and pieces break off, but this is not enough to destroy the rocky intruder. It still measures at least 6 miles (10 km) across.

Hurtling in from deep space at up to 60,000 mph (100,000 kph), the meteorite is a massive chunk of rock or metal. It is on a collision course with Earth and nothing can deflect it from its path—or prevent the imminent destruction.

meteorite A lump of space rock or metal that hits the surface of Earth. Usually from asteroids—larger chunks that circle the Sun.

extinct When a plant or animal species dies out and disappears completely.

friction When one object or surface rubs against another, producing heat.

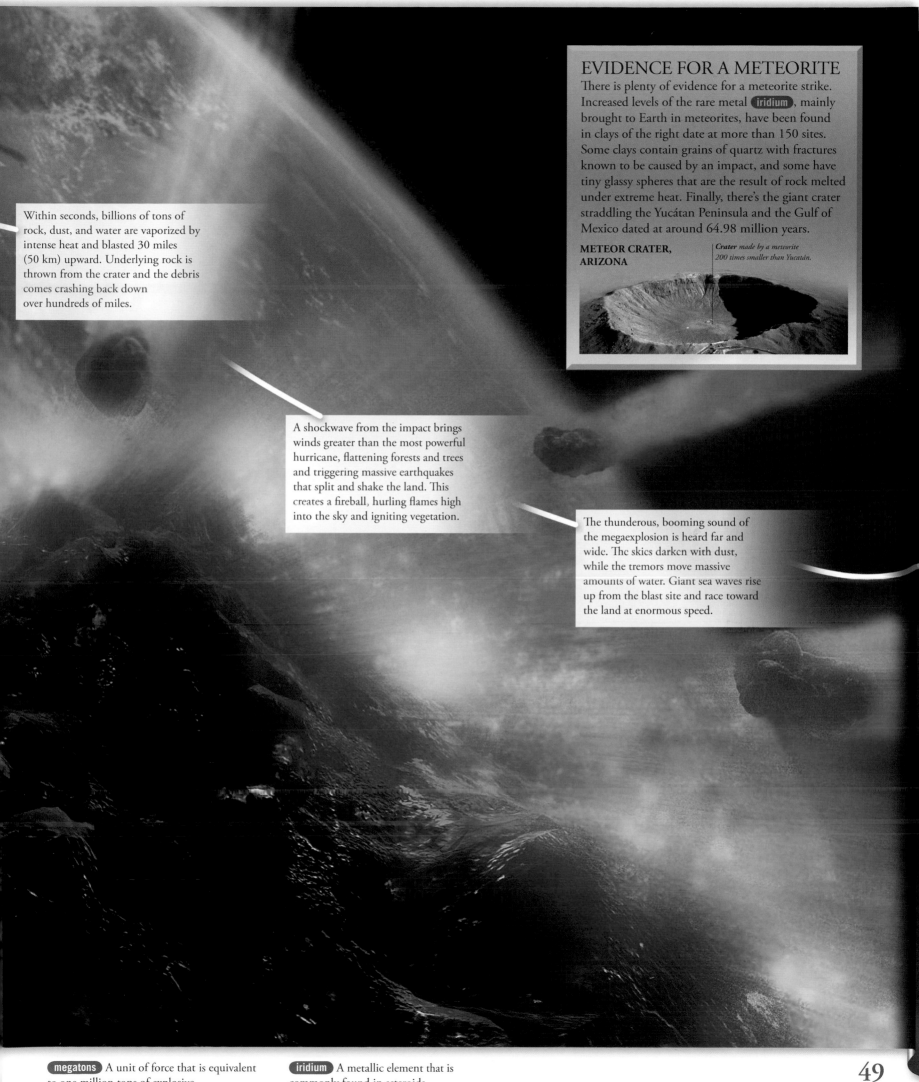

Within seconds, billions of tons of rock, dust, and water are vaporized by intense heat and blasted 30 miles (50 km) upward. Underlying rock is thrown from the crater and the debris comes crashing back down over hundreds of miles.

A shockwave from the impact brings winds greater than the most powerful hurricane, flattening forests and trees and triggering massive earthquakes that split and shake the land. This creates a fireball, hurling flames high into the sky and igniting vegetation.

The thunderous, booming sound of the megaexplosion is heard far and wide. The skies darken with dust, while the tremors move massive amounts of water. Giant sea waves rise up from the blast site and race toward the land at enormous speed.

EVIDENCE FOR A METEORITE

There is plenty of evidence for a meteorite strike. Increased levels of the rare metal **iridium**, mainly brought to Earth in meteorites, have been found in clays of the right date at more than 150 sites. Some clays contain grains of quartz with fractures known to be caused by an impact, and some have tiny glassy spheres that are the result of rock melted under extreme heat. Finally, there's the giant crater straddling the Yucátan Peninsula and the Gulf of Mexico dated at around 64.98 million years.

METEOR CRATER, ARIZONA

Crater made by a meteorite 200 times smaller than Yucatán.

megatons A unit of force that is equivalent to one million tons of explosive.

iridium A metallic element that is commonly found in asteroids, meteorites, and space dust.

High above the drowned coasts, a plume of red-hot debris rises skyward from the impact site. Winds disperse its burning contents across to dry land, and a million fire bombs fall like rain, starting firestorms that burn out of control.

Within days, dust from the explosion has traveled around the world, carried by high-speed winds. Billions of tons of dust and smoke particles are carried aloft in the atmosphere, shrouding the planet in a dirty, gray blanket that blocks out sunlight.

Giant walls of water called **tsunamis** reach the shallows, and their height increases as they draw water back from the beaches. Like the forces that caused them, they too are unstoppable, and they sweep far inland, washing away all in their path.

The Sun's light struggles to penetrate the global dust cloud. Temperatures drop and the planet enters a lengthy period of winter. Light levels fall, plants die, and animals that survived the blast, floods, and forest fires now face new dangers.

tsunamis Huge sea waves that are triggered by underwater earthquakes and volcanoes, or by massive landslides.

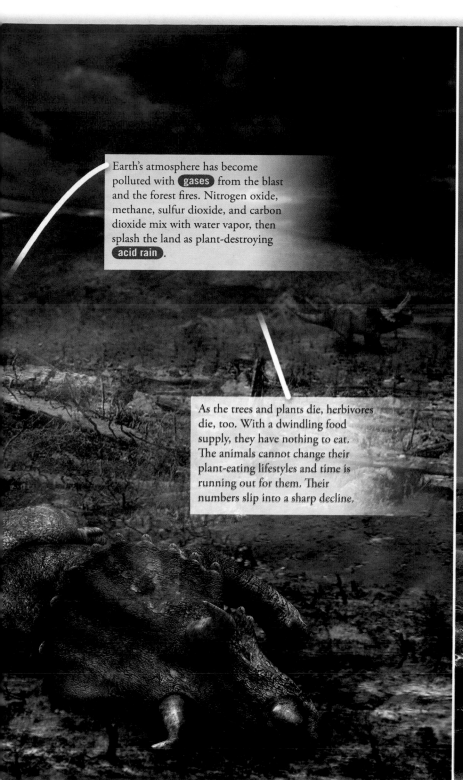

Earth's atmosphere has become polluted with **gases** from the blast and the forest fires. Nitrogen oxide, methane, sulfur dioxide, and carbon dioxide mix with water vapor, then splash the land as plant-destroying **acid rain**.

As the trees and plants die, herbivores die, too. With a dwindling food supply, they have nothing to eat. The animals cannot change their plant-eating lifestyles and time is running out for them. Their numbers slip into a sharp decline.

Even after the dust settles, high carbon dioxide levels remain in the atmosphere, raising the temperature to the sweltering heat of a greenhouse. With fewer herbivores to hunt, *Tyrannosaurus rex* and the other carnivores face a hungry future.

Although many of the effects of the meteorite strike were instantaneous, it takes many years for the full consequences to be felt. Meanwhile *Tyrannosaurus rex*, along with the other weak creatures left on Earth, is struggling to survive.

DEATH OF THE DINOSAURS

At the time of the meteorite strike, other environmental changes were taking place. Increased volcanic activity, with major eruptions in India, caused the atmosphere to become heavily polluted with dust particles, making it harder for the Sun's heat and light to reach the ground. Meanwhile poisonous sulfur fumes choked the air. It is also clear that huge climate changes were taking place and Earth was cooling. These events were once thought to be the sole cause of the dinosaurs' extinction, but now scientists agree that the impact was the main cause.

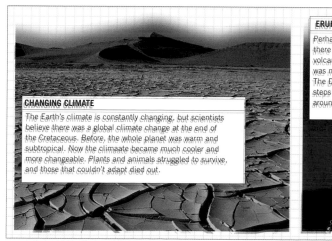

CHANGING CLIMATE

The Earth's climate is constantly changing, but scientists believe there was a global climate change at the end of the Cretaceous. Before, the whole planet was warm and subtropical. Now the climate became much cooler and more changeable. Plants and animals struggled to survive, and those that couldn't adapt died out.

ERUPTING VOLCANOES

Perhaps a supervolcano erupted, or maybe there was a series of eruptions from many volcanoes. Evidence has shown that there was major volcanic activity at the time. The Deccan Traps, in India, are steep steps of solidified lava that formed around 65 million years ago.

gases These form during the combustion, or burning, process or from decomposing plant and animal matter.

acid rain Rain that contains chemicals and is a weak acid. This can change the balance of the soil, killing trees and plants.

The ground turns to mud, streams become rivers, and animals caught unaware fall victim to the great flood that sweeps the land. Weak from hunger, *Tyrannosaurus rex* stumbles on the slippery ground and falls into the river.

With legs kicking, tail flicking, and jaws open wide, *Tyrannosaurus rex* struggles to free itself. Its scrambles are unheard against the deafening roar. The huge animal is swept along in the fast-flowing river of polluted and toxic floodwater.

Far from the metorite blast site, a lone *Tyrannosaurus rex* wanders across a ruined landscape. The pool where once it stalked its prey is a sheet of poisonous liquid. The sky sheds its load of black rain, each drop heavy with dust from the explosion.

FROM BONE TO STONE
The natural process of preserving the remains of an animal or plant is called fossilization. It can take thousands of years for a fossil to be made, during which time the remains are turned to stone. Most dinosaur fossils are the result of **permineralization**, which is what happens when bones, teeth, and claws are soaked in **minerals** in water. As the water trickles through the ground, it dissolves the remains to leave a dinosaur-shaped hole. In time, the hole may fill with **sediment** that sets into stone. The result is a **cast fossil**.

Archaeopteryx fossil

permineralization When minerals permeate, or spread through, the hard parts of a body—the skeleton, teeth, and nails.

minerals Substances that occur naturally in the ground that are neither plant nor animal, such as coal or stone.

sediment Fine particles, such as sand and silt, carried in water.

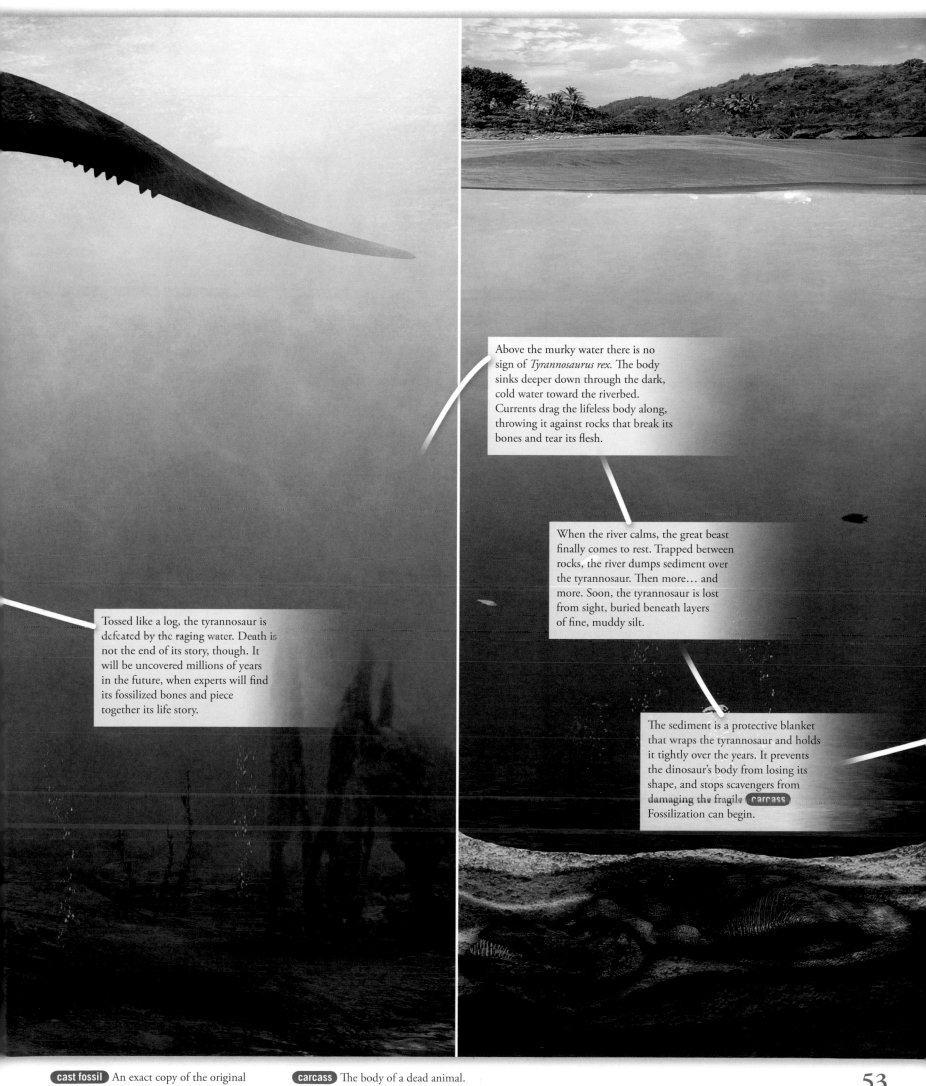

Above the murky water there is no sign of *Tyrannosaurus rex*. The body sinks deeper down through the dark, cold water toward the riverbed. Currents drag the lifeless body along, throwing it against rocks that break its bones and tear its flesh.

When the river calms, the great beast finally comes to rest. Trapped between rocks, the river dumps sediment over the tyrannosaur. Then more… and more. Soon, the tyrannosaur is lost from sight, buried beneath layers of fine, muddy silt.

Tossed like a log, the tyrannosaur is defeated by the raging water. Death is not the end of its story, though. It will be uncovered millions of years in the future, when experts will find its fossilized bones and piece together its life story.

The sediment is a protective blanket that wraps the tyrannosaur and holds it tightly over the years. It prevents the dinosaur's body from losing its shape, and stops scavengers from damaging the fragile **carcass**. Fossilization can begin.

cast fossil An exact copy of the original plant or animal, formed by replacing it with hardened minerals.

carcass The body of a dead animal.

53

Centuries pass by. The skeleton lies beneath ever-thickening layers of sediment. They press down and distort the shape of its bones. Little by little, the bones are dissolved by water, and mineral-rich sediments take their place.

The dinosaur's soft tissues are the first to change. **Microorganisms** attack its flesh and muscle, which rot away and expose the skeleton—it is this part of the tyrannosaur that will become a fossil. Above the bones, the riverbed is also slowly changing.

Mountains now stand where the river once flowed, raised up by the movement of the world's **continental plates** inching their way across the surface of the planet. Where plates collide, jagged mountains are pushed skyward.

Deep inside the mountain the tyrannosaur fossil is preserved in a tightly packed covering of rock. The sediments that filled the spaces where its bones used to be have set hard. They have formed a perfect cast, or copy, of the original specimen.

54

microsorganisms Tiny animals, such as bacteria, which are invisible to the human eye.

continental plates The pieces of the Earth's surface, or crust, which carry ocean and land.

SHAPING THE EARTH

Erosion can happen suddenly, such as when a storm sweeps away a beach at the coast, or over thousands of years, by the action of weather. Water from the sea, rivers, and rain washes against the coast and over land, altering the shape as it washes material away. Glaciers push their way down mountains and cut deep into the ground to form valleys. High winds blow abrasive material through the air and blast it against rock, wearing it down.

Crevasses created by ice at Tellot glacier, Canada

Paleontologists are surveying the area, and their expert eyes are quick to recognize the bones of a large theropod exposed in a rocky **bluff**. They hope it is a *Tyrannosaurus rex*. It would be the find of a lifetime.

As the forces bite into the rock, the ancient river sediments are worn away. The old rock gives up its secrets. Fossils of long dead animals may be found in place, but if erosion continues, the sections will scatter downhill and spread far apart.

Nothing lasts forever, not even mountains. Water, wind, and ice take their toll, wearing away their jaggedness and smoothing out their peaks. This is the nonstop action of **erosion**, which changes the look of the landscape.

erosion The wearing away of the land surface by natural forces.

bluff A steep cliff or riverbank.

55

CATALOG OF AN EXCAVATION

The excavation of a large dinosaur fossil is a slow and painstaking process. If Barnum Brown, excavator of the first *Tyrannosaurus rex* back in 1902, could see today's paleontologists at work, he would recognize some of their tools and techniques, but he would probably be amazed by the differences. Modern excavation involves studying both the skeleton and its surroundings and keeping careful records of the site for clues about the dinosaur's life.

Locating the find spot

The location of the site—known as the find spot—is accurately mapped with a global positioning satellite (GPS) for map references and a compass for directions. This helps paleontologists to create a distribution map of fossil sites over a wide area.

Compass

Geological map

Tape measure

Kneeling mat

Spoil bucket

Excavation tools

After the overburden (the mass of rock on top of the find) has been removed, a variety of hand tools are used to chip and scrape away material closer to the bones. Sieving the debris recovers small finds that could easily be missed.

Rock hammer

Picks and scrapers

Sieve

Pointing trowel　*Brush*　*Brush*

Rock chisels with hand protectors　*Lump hammer*　*Worn trowel*

When tools wear down

After a few days' use, tools such as chisels and trowels are worn down by the rock. Their steel blades quickly lose their point and edge. When this happens, they cease to be useful and need to be replaced.

Mapping the site

A grid of string divides the site into small squares. A draftsman then makes an accurate pencil drawing of the fossil, showing how it lies in the ground. The grid squares on the ground match the squares on the paper.

Grid square

On the site

Many people are involved in the excavation. The team is led by a site director, who is often from a university or a museum and a paleontologist or expert in dinosaur studies. Other people in the team include photographers, draftsmen, surveyors, and diggers. Together, they contribute to building up a detailed record of the site, which can be examined later for clues about the dinosaur's life.

Making the site drawing

Fossil bones

Drawing frame

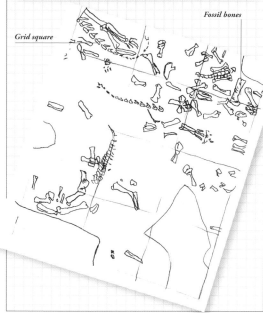

Plan view of site

The pencil site drawings are inked in later on. As each drawing is completed, it is joined to its neighboring drawing, until a plan view of the whole site has been produced. It shows the articulation (position) of the skeleton.

Grid square

Fossil bones

Plaster field jacket

After the bones have been drawn and photograped, they are wrapped in a plaster jacket. This protects them during the lifting process, when they are freed from the bedrock, and also for their trip back to the museum or laboratory.

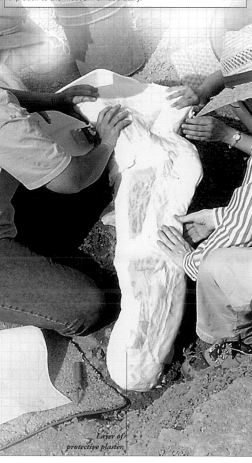

Layer of protective plaster

The fossilized skeleton of *Tyrannosaurus rex* comes to the surface after its covering of rock is weathered away. A team of paleontologists conducts an excavation to uncover its bones. They map and photograph them still in position in the ground.

Over thousands of years, the natural movement of the ground can make the rock rise, fall, buckle, and fold, causing its layers to split and shift. If this happens, a fossilized skeleton will become **disarticulated** as its bones become scattered.

Most of the bones are kept in the surrounding blocks of rock when they are taken from the **field site** and transported to a museum. Fossils that are exposed and fragile are protected with a thick coating of plaster, to hold them together.

TYRANNOSAUR REBORN

For 65 million years the fossilized skeleton of *Tyrannosaurus rex* lay entombed within a protecting cloak of solid rock. The dinosaur's remains had been hidden away by the forces of nature, and it was nature that finally reached down and exposed the long-buried fossil. Glaciers scraped over the ground surface and rivers cut across the landscape. They both sliced valleys deep into the **bedrock**. Blasted by wind, lashed by rain, and shattered by frost, the ancient rock was reduced to grains of sand. Eventually the nonstop action of erosion would have scattered this skeleton, or worn the bones away, but this tyranosaur has been spotted by fossil hunters and saved by science.

IN THE LABORATORY

At the museum laboratory, the preparators have the painstaking job of freeing the fossils from the rock. Saws and drills cut away large chunks, then **scribe tools** carefully crumble away the last of the rock. The original dinosaur fossils are rarely put on display, as they are too valuable or fragile. They are kept in storerooms and made available to scientists.

Cleaning a *T. rex* jawbone

bedrock The solid rock that lies beneath top loose soil, sand, clay, pebbles, and gravel.

disarticulated Mixed up and no longer in the correct position.

field site The place where the fossils were discovered and excavated—dug up fom the ground.

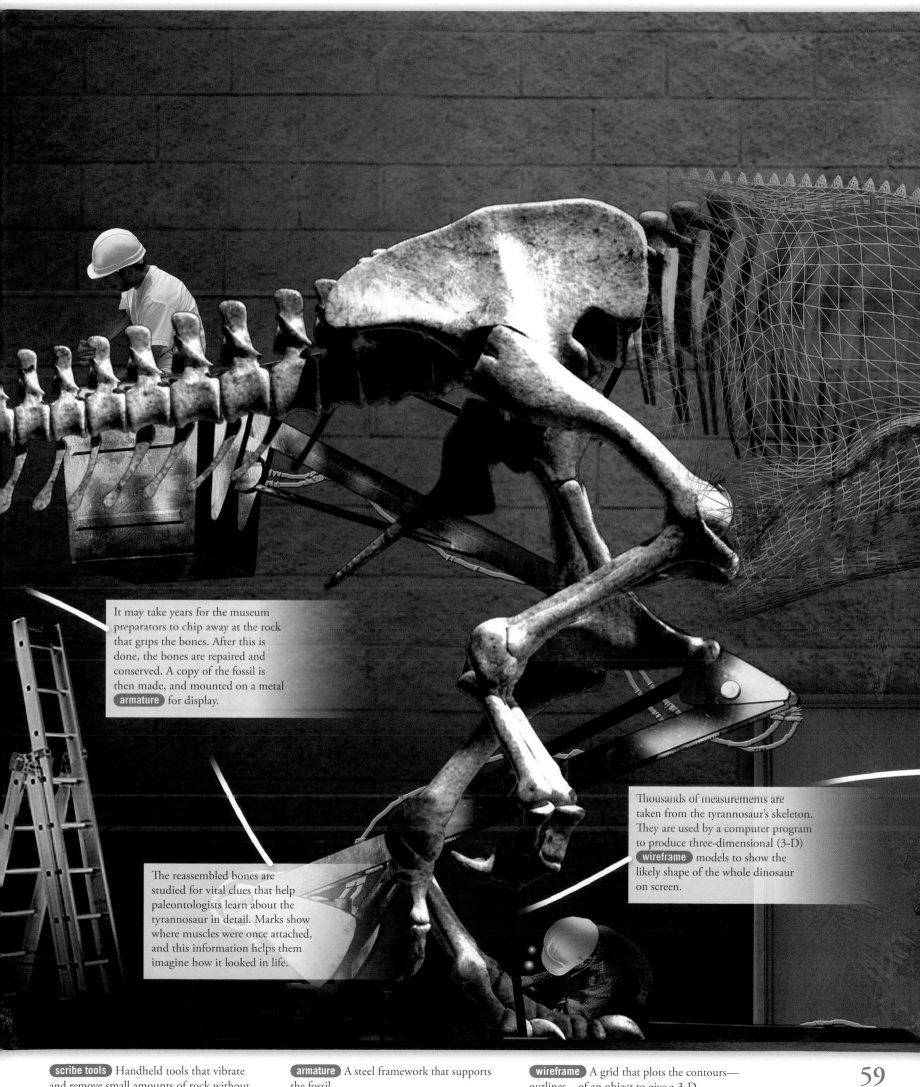

It may take years for the museum preparators to chip away at the rock that grips the bones. After this is done, the bones are repaired and conserved. A copy of the fossil is then made, and mounted on a metal **armature** for display.

Thousands of measurements are taken from the tyrannosaur's skeleton. They are used by a computer program to produce three-dimensional (3-D) **wireframe** models to show the likely shape of the whole dinosaur on screen.

The reassembled bones are studied for vital clues that help paleontologists learn about the tyrannosaur in detail. Marks show where muscles were once attached, and this information helps them imagine how it looked in life.

scribe tools Handheld tools that vibrate and remove small amounts of rock without pressure having to be applied.

armature A steel framework that supports the fossil.

wireframe A grid that plots the contours—outlines—of an object to give a 3-D representation of it.

The first skin is completely smooth. To make it look more lifelike, a texture is added to re-create the pebbly skin that *Tyrannosaurus rex* is thought to have had. This is based on fossilized skin impressions that have been discovered.

Next, color is added to the computerized image. Fossils don't show the dinosaurs' original colors and markings, so they are matched to modern animals, such as crocodiles, elephants, and rhinos. Eyes, teeth, and claws are then added.

The wireframe 3-D computer model puts flesh on the bones, precisely following its skeletal and muscular structure to reveal the shape of the dinosaur's body. Then a computer-generated skin is stretched over the wireframe.

Animators can now set the computer model moving, based on the range of movement each bone joint would have allowed, and on reconstructed muscles. By watching modern animals they can also work out how smoothly *T. rex* moved and how it balanced.

skin impressions Skin prints formed by a dead dinosaur in the surrounding mud, which can harden and survive as fossils.

Some scientists think a few species of dinosaurs were able to **evolve**. In fact, most scientists now agree that birds evolved from feathered dinosaurs. Fossil evidence reveals that some of the smaller theropods had featherlike structures on their bodies.

DINOSAURS AS BIRDS

During the 1990s, paleontologists found fossils in China that confirmed a link between dinosaurs and birds. *Caudipteryx* (meaning "Tail Feather"), *Sinosauropteryx* ("Chinese Winged Lizard"), and *Mononykus* ("Single Claw") were bird-sized theropods whose skeletons are almost identical to those of birds.

Wishbone adds strength to support wings

Furcula, or wishbone, is similar to modern birds' wishbones

Skeleton of a modern sea eagle

Mononykus **skeleton from the Cretaceous**

What about larger therapods—did they have feathers? An early member of the tyrannosaur family, *Dilong paradoxus*, was recently found to have had a feathery coat. So next time you see a bird fly by, think of a long-ago hunter called *Tyrannosaurus rex*.

A 3-D background is created to show the late-Cretaceous landscape, and sound effects are added to match the scene. With the aid of computers, modern science has brought *T. rex* back to life with a roar, 65 million years after it became extinct.

evolve To develop, or change, gradually over many years.

ATLAS OF FOSSIL FINDS

Fossils of dinosaurs and other prehistoric reptiles have been found on every continent, even Antarctica. Almost 1,000 different species have been identified—probably a fraction of the number that once lived on Earth. Some are named after the person who discovered them, some get their names from the place where they were found, and others are given names that describe their physical appearance.

NORTH AMERICA

Tyrannosaurus rex

Triceratops

Hadrosaurus

Diplodocus

Stegosaurus

Coelophysis

Baryonyx

Iguanodon

Hypsilophodon

Spinosaurus

Saltasaurus

SOUTH AMERICA

Herrerasaurus

Lesothosaurus

Giganotosaurus

Mussaurus

ANTARCTICA

North America

Some of the best-known dinosaurs come from the United States and Canada. In the western US, where the climate is dry and there is little vegetation and much bare rock, erosion has worn the rock away, exposing the fossils buried inside. Since the 1850s, the continent's dinosaurs have been collected and studied and North America is now home to some of the world's leading dinosaur experts and museums.

Diplodocus

South America

It was only in the 1950s that paleontologists turned their attention to finding dinosaurs in South America. Since then, more than 50 different species have been identified. Among these are *Eoraptor* ("Dawn Thief"), one of the first dinosaurs to appear around 228 million years ago, and *Giganotosaurus* ("Giant Southern Lizard"), a megacarnivore bigger than *Tyrannosaurus rex*.

Giganotosaurus

Marine Reptiles

While dinosaurs ruled the land, several orders of marine reptiles, including mosasaurs, ichthyosaurs, nothosaurs, and plesiosaurs, ruled the sea at different times. The fossilized remains of these prehistoric aquatic reptiles are found today on dry land, giving clear evidence for the changing shape of the Earth's continents and for higher sea levels in the past. Unlike the dinosaurs, their closest relatives are lizards and turtles.

Tylosaurus was a mosasaur, one of the oldest marine reptiles, whose fossils have been found in North America and New Zealand. It had a hard, bony snout, which was probably used as a ramming weapon to stun its prey.

Elasmosaurus was the largest of the plesiosaurs—an enormous 46 ft (14 m) long. Its fossils have been found in North America. The huge muscles that powered its flippers were anchored to large, platelike shoulder bones.

Ichthyosaurus belonged to the ichthyosaurs. Its fossils have been found across the Atlantic and came in all sizes. This sharklike creature had extremely large eyes, which may have helped it to hunt in the murky depths.

Peloneustes was a member of the pliosaur family, which was part of the plesiosaur order. Its fossils have been found across Europe. Its short neck and streamlined body most closely resembles modern whales.

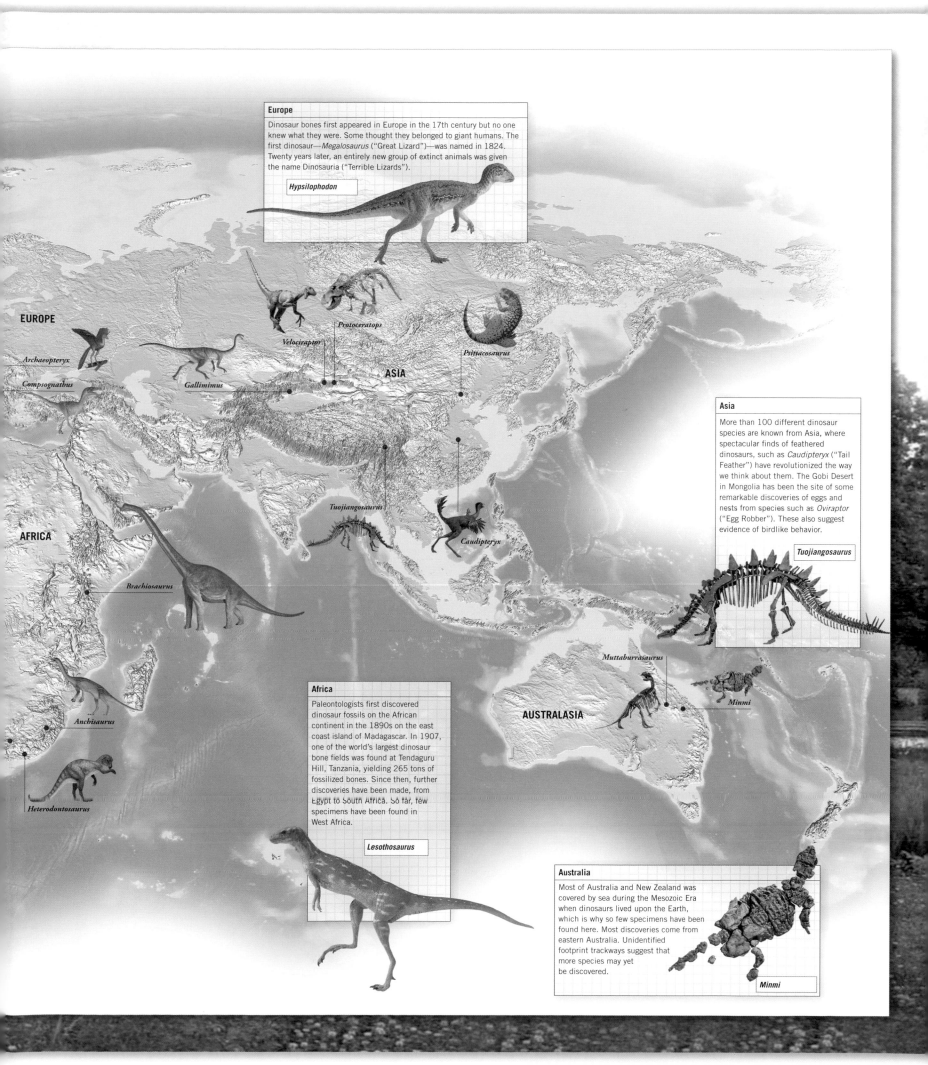

Europe

Dinosaur bones first appeared in Europe in the 17th century but no one knew what they were. Some thought they belonged to giant humans. The first dinosaur—*Megalosaurus* ("Great Lizard")—was named in 1824. Twenty years later, an entirely new group of extinct animals was given the name Dinosauria ("Terrible Lizards").

Hypsilophodon

EUROPE

Archaeopteryx

Compsognathus

Velociraptor

Protoceratops

Gallimimus

ASIA

Psittacosaurus

Asia

More than 100 different dinosaur species are known from Asia, where spectacular finds of feathered dinosaurs, such as *Caudipteryx* ("Tail Feather") have revolutionized the way we think about them. The Gobi Desert in Mongolia has been the site of some remarkable discoveries of eggs and nests from species such as *Oviraptor* ("Egg Robber"). These also suggest evidence of birdlike behavior.

Tuojiangosaurus

Tuojiangosaurus

Caudipteryx

AFRICA

Brachiosaurus

Muttaburrasaurus

Minmi

AUSTRALASIA

Anchisaurus

Africa

Paleontologists first discovered dinosaur fossils on the African continent in the 1890s on the east coast island of Madagascar. In 1907, one of the world's largest dinosaur bone fields was found at Tendaguru Hill, Tanzania, yielding 265 tons of fossilized bones. Since then, further discoveries have been made, from Egypt to South Africa. So far, few specimens have been found in West Africa.

Heterodontosaurus

Lesothosaurus

Australia

Most of Australia and New Zealand was covered by sea during the Mesozoic Era when dinosaurs lived upon the Earth, which is why so few specimens have been found here. Most discoveries come from eastern Australia. Unidentified footprint trackways suggest that more species may yet be discovered.

Minmi

63

DINOSAUR CLASSIFICATION

In 1842, the renowned British anatomist Sir Richard Owen announced the existence of a new order of extinct animals, Dinosauria ("Terrible Lizards"). In 1887, another British scientist, Harry Seeley, divided this group into two distinct kinds, based on the shape of their hip bones. His system is still used today.

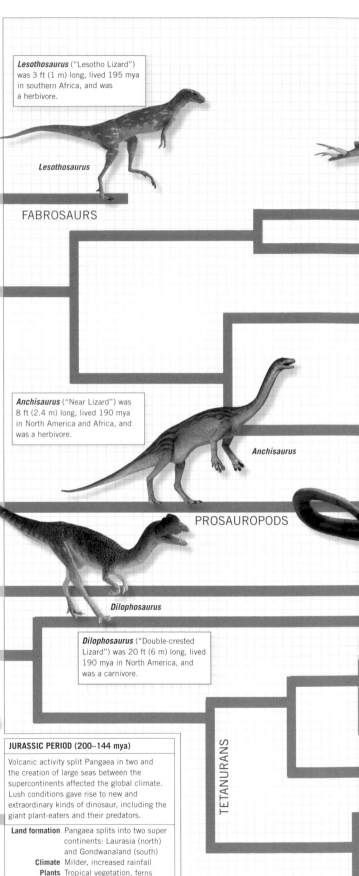

Lesothosaurus ("Lesotho Lizard") was 3 ft (1 m) long, lived 195 mya in southern Africa, and was a herbivore.

Lesothosaurus

FABROSAURS

Anchisaurus ("Near Lizard") was 8 ft (2.4 m) long, lived 190 mya in North America and Africa, and was a herbivore.

Anchisaurus

PROSAUROPODS

Dilophosaurus

Dilophosaurus ("Double-crested Lizard") was 20 ft (6 m) long, lived 190 mya in North America, and was a carnivore.

TETANURANS

TRIASSIC PERIOD (250–200 mya)

The Triassic Period marked the start of the dinosaur era, known as the Mesozoic Era. The earliest dinosaurs were small meat-eaters and much larger plant-eaters that could walk on two or four legs. Fossils of the first dinosaurs have been found all over the world.

Land formation	Earth consists of a single landmass known as Pangaea
Climate	Constant warm temperature
Plants	Conifers, cycads, shrubs
Dinosaurs	*Eoraptor, Plateosaurus*
Reptiles	Pterosaurs (air), Ichthyosaurs (sea)

Ornithischians

Dinosaurs in this group have hip bones shaped like modern birds, with both pelvis bones pointing backward. Despite their name, there is no evolutionary link between this group and birds.

ORNITHISCHIANS

Coelophysis ("Hollow Form") was 10 ft (3 m) long, lived 220 million years ago in North America, and was a carnivore.

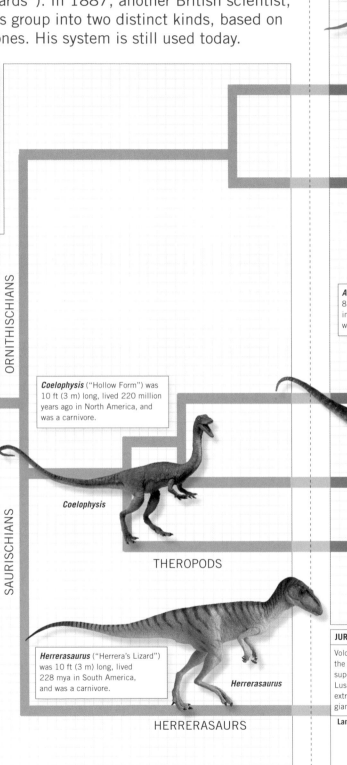

Coelophysis

Saurischians

Dinosaurs in this group have hip bones shaped like modern lizards, with one bone pointing forward (the pubis) and the other pointing backward (the ischium). Birds most probably evolved from small feathered theropods.

SAURISCHIANS

THEROPODS

Herrerasaurus ("Herrera's Lizard") was 10 ft (3 m) long, lived 228 mya in South America, and was a carnivore.

Herrerasaurus

HERRERASAURS

JURASSIC PERIOD (200–144 mya)

Volcanic activity split Pangaea in two and the creation of large seas between the supercontinents affected the global climate. Lush conditions gave rise to new and extraordinary kinds of dinosaur, including the giant plant-eaters and their predators.

Land formation	Pangaea splits into two super continents: Laurasia (north) and Gondwanaland (south)
Climate	Milder, increased rainfall
Plants	Tropical vegetation, ferns
Dinosaurs	*Diplodocus, Allosaurus*
Reptiles	Plesiosaurs (sea)

TRIASSIC

JURASSIC

Stegosaurus ("Roofed Lizard") was 30 ft (9 m) long, lived 150 mya in North America, and was a herbivore.

Stegosaurus

CRETACEOUS PERIOD (144–65 mya)

Wet and dry seasons led to the appearance of flowering plants and large forests, which supported vast numbers of plant-eaters. The sheer variety and numbers of dinosaurs marked the highpoint of their development. Cretaceous was the end of the Mesozoic Era.

Land formation	Supercontinents continue to split into recognizable continents
Climate	Summer and winter seasons
Plants	Angiosperms (flowering plants)
Dinosaurs	*Saltasaurus*, *Tyrannosaurus rex*
Reptiles	Snakes (land)

Euoplocephalus ("Well-armored Head") was 20 ft (6 m) long, lived 70 mya in North America, and was a herbivore.

Euoplocephalus

STEGOSAURS

ANKYLOSAURS

Iguanodon ("Iguana Tooth") was 33 ft (10 m) long, lived 130 mya in Europe and North America, and was a herbivore.

Iguanodon

Pachycephalosaurus ("Thick-headed Lizard") was 15 ft (4.6 m) long, lived 70 mya in North America, and was a herbivore.

ORNITHOPODS

Pachycephalosaurus

PACHYCEPHALOSAURS

Triceratops ("Three-horned Face") was 30 ft (9 m) long, lived 70 mya in North America, and was a herbivore.

Triceratops

MARGINOCEPHALIANS

CERATOPSIANS

Barosaurus ("Heavy Lizard") was 90 ft (27 m) long, lived 150 mya in North America and Africa, and was a herbivore.

Barosaurus

Deinonychus ("Terrible Claw") was 10 ft (3 m) long, lived 113 mya in North America, and was a carnivore.

SAUROPODS

COELOPHYSIDS AND CERATOSAURS

Deinonychus

Archaeopteryx ("Ancient Wing") was 2 ft (60 cm) long, lived 150 mya in Europe, and was a carnivore.

DROMAEOSAURS

Archaeopteryx

Auquila rapax

Tyrannosaurus rex ("King of the Tyrant Lizards") was 40 ft (12 m) long, lived 70 mya in North America, and was a carnivore.

Tyrannosaurus rex

BIRDS

Aquila rapax ("Tawny Eagle") is 2 ft (70 cm) long, lives in Africa and Asia, and is a carnivore. Shares similar features to small theropods.

TYRANNOSAURS

Giganotosaurus

Giganotosaurus ("Giant Southern Lizard") was 52 ft (16 m) long, lived 100 mya in South America, and was a carnivore.

ALLOSAURS

Baryonyx ("Heavy Claw") was 33 ft (10 m) long, lived 120 mya in Europe, and was a carnivore.

Baryonyx

SPINOSAURS

CRETACEOUS

INDEX

ACKNOWLEDGMENTS

Dorling Kindersley would like to thank Lynn Bresler for proofreading and the index, and Margaret Parrish for text Americanization.

Picture Credits

The publisher would like to thank the following for their kind permission to reproduce their photographs:

(Abbreviations key: (t) = top, (b) = bottom, (tl) = top left), (bl) = bottom left, (tr) = top right, (br) = bottom right, (tc) = top center, (bc) = bottom center, (bcr) = bottom center right, (bcl) = bottom center left, (cra) = center right above, (crb) = center right below), (cla) = center left above, (clb) = center left below.)

4–5: Peter Larson/©1990 BHIGR; 6: Bettmann/Corbis; 7: Bettmann/Corbis (b); 19: Louie Psihoyos/Stone Company.com Inc (br); 20 : Mick Ellison (tl); 22 :DK Images/ Courtesy of the American Museum of Natural History (tl), DK Images/Courtesy of the American Museum of Natural History (tc), Danny Lehman/Corbis (tr), The Field Museum (bl), Royal Saskatchewan Museum (bc), The Field Museum (br); 23: DK Images/Courtesy of the Natural History Museum, London (tl), DK Images/ Courtesy of the Royal Tyrrell Museum of Palaeontology, Alberta, Canada (bl); 27: 'Science' (b); 28: Ed Gerken/© 1996 BHIGR (t); 29: The Field Museum (br); 30: The Field Museum (tr), Peter Larson/©1990 BHIGR (bl); 30–31: Peter Larson/©1990 BHIGR (b); 31: Peter Larson/©1990 BHIGR (tr), The Field Museum (br); 34: Tom Bean/Corbis (tl); 36: DK Images/ Courtesy of the Royal Tyrrell Museum of Palaeontology, Alberta, Canada (bl); 37: DK Images/Courtesy of the American Museum of Natural History (bl), DK Images/Courtesy of the American Museum of Natural History (bcr); 41: DK Images/Courtesy of the Natural History Museum, London (br); 45: DK Images/Courtesy of the Natural History Museum, London (tl), DK Images/Jonathon Hateley (b); 46: Science Photo Library/Prof. Walter Alvarez (t), Science Photo Library/Alfred Pasieka (bl), Roger Ressmeyer/Corbis (br); 47: Science Photo Library/Geological Survey of Canada (t), G Larson (b); 49: Charles and Josette Lenars/Corbis (tr); 51: Altrendo/Getty Images (bl), Image Bank/Getty Images (br); 52: Science Photo Library/Hervé Conge, ISM (br); 55: Science Photo Library/David Nunuk (tl); 56: Nate Murphy/Judith River Dinosaur Institute (br); 56-57: Nate Murphy/Judith River Dinosaur Institute (b); 57: Nate Murphy/Judith River Dinosaur Institute (br); 58: Corbis (br); 61: Corbis/Louie Psihoyos (inset left), Natural History Museum, London (inset right); 62: DK Images/Graham High, Centaur Studios (tl), DK Images/Courtesy of the Natural History Museum, London (cr), DK Images/Roby Braun (clb), DK Images/Roby Braun (crb); 63: DK Images/Graham High, Centaur Studios (cla), DK Images/Courtesy of the Natural History Museum, London (cr), DK Images/Courtesy of the Natural History Museum, London (cra), DK Images/Roby Braun (bc), DK Images/Courtesy of Queensland Museum, Brisbane, Australia (br); DK Images/Roby Braun (clb); 64: DK Images/Roby Braun (tr), DK Images/Roby Braun (cb), DK Images/Roby Braun (cr), DK Images/Roby Braun (cra); 65: DK Images/Courtesy of the Natural History Museum, London (bl), DK Images/Centaur Studios (b), DK Images/Courtesy of the National Birds of Prey Centre, Gloucestershire (br).

All other images © Dorling Kindersley.
For further information see: www.dkimages.com

Every effort has been made to trace all copyright holders. The publisher will be pleased to hear from any copyright holders not here acknowledged.

LONDON, NEW YORK, MELBOURNE,
MUNICH, AND DELHI

Consultant Professor Michael Benton

Senior Editor Julie Ferris
Senior Art Editor Owen Peyton Jones
Editors Jayne Miller, Nigel Ritchie
Designers Jacqui Swan, Johnny Pau
DTP Coordinator Andy Hilliard

Managing Editor Camilla Hallinan
Managing Art Editor Sophia M. Tampakopoulos Turner

Publishing Managers Caroline Buckingham, Andrew Macintyre
Category Publishers Laura Buller, Jonathan Metcalf

Picture Research Sarah Hopper, Rose Horridge, Jo Walton
Production Erica Rosen
Jacket Design Neal Cobourne

Illustrators pixel-shack

First American Edition, 2006

Published in the United States by
DK Publishing, Inc.
375 Hudson Street
New York, New York 10014

06 07 08 09 10 10 9 8 7 6 5 4 3 2 1

A Cataloging-in-Publication record for this book is available from the Library of Congress.

ISBN-10 0-7566-1412-0
ISBN-13 978-0-7566-1412-6

Color reproduction by Colourscan, Singapore
Printed and bound in China by Hung Hing

Discover more at
www.dk.com